A Summer in '68

Dee Davidson Dosch

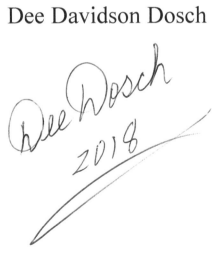

Strategic Book Publishing and Rights Co.

Strategic Book Publishing and Rights Co., LLC
USA | Singapore
www.sbpra.com

For information about special discounts for bulk purchases, please contact Strategic Book Publishing and Rights Co. Special Sales, at bookorder@sbpra.net.

ISBN: 978-1-948858-63-2

Book Design: Suzanne Kelly

This story is dedicated to all the kids I loved in the summer of '68 and especially Nancy Moore.

Acknowledgements

This is my second memoir and I would like to thank all the friends and family who kept asking me for several years when I was going to write another book or I would never have attempted to compose this second story.

My immediate, as well as my extended family and close friends, both current and past, were always in my thoughts as I wrote from the notes of a journal written fifty years ago during my summer of 1968. Just like with my first book, *A Summer in '69*, none of it would have been possible without the funding and blessings of my mom and dad, who allowed me to spread my wings and experience time away from home to learn about myself and others.

My summer in 1968 was similar to my summer in 1969 in that it was full of adventure, exploring, travel surprises, and brief romances. While reading my journal account, reminiscing, researching, and studying for the manuscript, I was able to relive a time gone by but yet an extremely important period in the history of our country. For this I am grateful for the encouragement to proceed.

I especially appreciate my husband, Dr. John D. Hume, for the many hours he had to quietly retreat from my life when I had my nose buried in the computer for days. He has been my friend since first grade and knows all the good, bad, and ugly of his infamous partner. John is my biggest fan, and I could not accomplish half of what I do without his continued support and patience.

Lastly, to every person I mention in the book, I was touched in some way, whether briefly or long term, during this special time in my growing-up and maturing. I learned much about love and relationships, war and reconciliation, conviction and accep-

Dee Davidson Dosch

tance, happiness and compassion, sharing and trusting, friendship and morality. I'm indebted to all of those people for how they influenced the girl that I was to the woman that I became.

Introduction

In the summer of 1968, I spent three months working at a lodge in Estes Park, Colorado. I was only eighteen years old at the time and had just completed all the vitally required classes I had to take during my first year of college. Because I lived at home while going to school, my parents were not opposed to my leaving for a summer retreat since the job I contracted also provided room and board. I kept a daily journal during my stay, recording daily activities, thoughts, and current events both locally and nationally. Otherwise, I would not have been able to remember most of what this story chronicles.

The names of those I mention in the book have not been changed to protect their identity. I have not seen or spoken to most of these individuals in over fifty years. I purposely did not disclose the last names of those described except for a few who are probably no longer living or are public personalities. I was provided with a list of the names and addresses of the 1968 employees before I left the lodge. I kept this in my notebook or I wouldn't know most of the names revealed.

Arriving a few days later than my starting date at the Estes Park Chalet, my family stopped off on the way in Chanute, Kansas where my dad's youngest sister, Diana, was getting married.

We were all part of the wedding. My dad's mother had died a few weeks after he was born, but within a few years, my grandfather would marry my step-grandmother Millie. They went on to have four delightful daughters together. Diana was twenty years younger than her brother (my dad) and a few years older than me. The ceremony was enchanting with traditional nuptials, including a lineup of over twenty family members. The maid of honor was her fiancé's sister, Loeva, and Phil's best man was his cousin Fred. The four bridesmaids were the other sisters, Pat, Peggy, Nancy, and yours truly. The four groomsmen included my father Frank and the husbands of the sisters, Carl, Red, and Ron. The two little flower girls were my darling cousins, Christy and Susan, and the two candle lighters were another cousin of mine, Gayla, and Charlotte, sister of the groom. My youngest cousin Kevin was the ring bearer and of the four ushers, two were my brothers, Chuck and Bill. Bill, by the way, missed his high school graduation to be there. Last, but not least, my beautiful mother Wannel sang, "Oh Perfect Love" and "The Wedding Prayer."

I know my aunt tried hard not to exclude anyone who might get their feelings hurt. She even let her other rowdy nephews, Paul, Larry, Bobby, Ricky, Randy, Rusty, Steve, Robert, Bruce, and Kirk distribute rice packets to the guests. It was truly a family affair with this clan!

I describe this special occasion to inform my readers about the kind of middle-class family I had the good fortune to be born in to and grew up spending my youthful years. Not quite a total WASP, (White, Anglo-Saxon, and Protestant) but almost. My Protestant raised parents converted to Catholicism when I started school. We were a close-knit, extended family that got together on the holidays since everyone lived in Missouri, Kansas, Oklahoma, or Texas. Even my mother's side of the family, which was much smaller, also lived in Oklahoma.

Despite the "normal" dysfunctional family dynamics we lived, everyone loved each other and would give the shirt off their back if needed. Being the only girl in a family of six children, you can just ask any of my brothers, and they will tell you I was spoiled and got my own bedroom.

But I was one of the "three big kids" so I had to help with my share of chores and assisting with the "three little kids." And by the way, like everyone else, I got hand-me-down outfits from my Aunt Diana until I started high school, and then I made my own clothes when Diana stopped growing. Yes, I could sew, but I didn't cook because my mom didn't want us underfoot when she was preparing meals. I never learned to cook much and really didn't care.

According to historians, 1968 was the year that "shattered" America. The year that was totally "out-of-control" and would never be the same. My story in 1968 is far away from the trauma, protests, disturbances, and devastation but it happened nonetheless. So, sit back and enjoy my personal memoir and the experiences I had that year in my true story of *A Summer In '68*.

Contents

Chapter One: Tuesday, June 4

My summer of 1968 began as I gazed out the car window at the breathtaking views of the Rocky Mountain National Park with snow still on the mountaintops on this first week in June.

I had loved this state since a trip I took with my family after my eighth-grade year in junior high when we visited Colorado Springs, drove through the Garden of the Gods, and up Pikes Peak.

We even panned for gold at the El Paso Gold Mine in Cripple Creek and crossed the bridge over the Royal Gorge. I knew then I wanted to return someday and live in what I considered to be God's country. Taking advantage of a student exchange program at my college, I applied for a seasonal position with accommodations. Although I'd have to lower my standards to cleaning rooms as a full-time maid for employment, I couldn't wait to get there as my parents drove me through the mountains to a small village located sixty miles northwest of Denver in Larimer County.

I had just finished my first year of college at Southwest Missouri State in my hometown of Springfield and was about to spend my summer break at a lodge close to Mary's Lake about two miles outside the busy tourist community of Estes Park. Missouri native Joel Estes, one of the earliest settlers, is who the town, which sits at 7,522 feet above sea level, is named. This popular summer resort area has been around since the turn of the century for both hikers and mountain climbers. The elevated lake surroundings where we ended up was in a rather secluded area, but it was an absolutely gorgeous location. The mountaintops were frosted with the winter snows, and you could feel the cool highland air as the sun set behind them as we reached our last stop.

After entering the hotel lobby and meeting the front desk supervisor, I hugged and waved goodbye to my parents and two youngest brothers, Larry and Robert, for the next three months. I was told by my dad I could call home on the holidays or in case of an emergency. Otherwise, I was to "behave and don't take any wooden nickels." They all headed back to town to find a cheaper place to stay. The chalet was not opened yet for paying customers anyway.

A staff member took me upstairs to the female employees' attic dormitory on the third floor, and she told me to report to the housekeeping staff supervisor at 7 a.m. Although the mountain lodge was big, beautiful, and rustic, the girl's residence rooms were not. The walls were white with an exposed hanging rod and shelf for clothes just to the right of the door as you entered the room.

A freestanding sink was next to the makeshift closet and on the other side of the room were the furnishings, two twin metal beds and an antique dresser with a mirror attached.

The only window was on the far side of the divided room and not within my view. A pay phone hung on the wall across the hallway next to the bathrooms and commodes. It was here that I could use as much toilet paper as I wanted. My dad, frugal to the point of being ridiculous at times, insisted his children only use four squares of tissues at a time. Me, being the obedient daughter that I was, followed his rules for fear of getting in trouble. Besides, it was one of the Ten Commandments to obey your parents. It didn't take me long to unpack and put away the outfits, shoes, and toiletries that I had brought along for my temporary summer dwelling.

My roommate had not yet arrived, but there was an adjoining room already occupied by two girls who were also from Missouri. I introduced myself to Janet A. from Louisiana and Gina S. from Sullivan. They let me know they were both students at Fontbonne College, a Catholic women's school in the St. Louis area. I told them I was also Catholic and that maybe we could

2

find a church nearby to go to Mass together on Sunday. Both of these gals were tall, thin, and attractive.

Gina had long, fiery red hair, and Janet was a brunette with a medium-length, flip-style haircut. I, on the other hand, was short, of medium build, and wore my dishwater-blond hair long and straight.

There was no TV or radio in the dorm rooms, but one of my roomies had thought to bring her record player so we listened to music while we talked. After sharing more family information and some personal stories about special relationships back home, we all got ready for bed. I was bushed after the long and tiresome drive through the flat state of Kansas.

As I lay there that night, I thought about both the guys I dated back home and wondered if I would hear from either one of them while being separated. Though we were not in a serious relationship, I cared about them both. I had dated Mike W. my senior year in high school, but after graduation, he decided to go away to a theology college to see if being a priest was his calling in life.

Although this was a rather awkward situation, I supported his decision, and he was off to Loras College Seminary in Dubuque, Iowa. Meanwhile, I started dating Ronnie T., another guy I liked in high school, but he was involved with someone else at the time. Mike had finished his first year away studying religion and had decided it was not his vocation after all. So, he was back in my life too, and I would be gone from both of them for the entire summer, two states away.

I elected not to go to breakfast the first morning since getting up at 6:00 a.m. in the morning barely gave me enough time to get ready to report for work duty at seven o'clock. The coed employee cafeteria on the first floor served three hot meals a day to the workers and staff. The first day on the job, learning to clean hotel rooms, was nothing remarkable. It was more of a training workshop on how to make beds with squared-off sheet corners and wrinkle-free linens.

Mrs. Mosley, the house cleaning day manager, was a middle-aged, gray-haired, heavy-set lady with a slight limp.

3

She instructed me on her rigid method of scrubbing sinks, counters, and toilets, as well as dusting furniture, sweeping, vacuuming, and mopping floors. The guests would arrive by the end of the week, and we were getting the rooms ready to be occupied. Once my roommate arrived, she and I would pair up together to be housekeeping partners.

A welcomed lunch break gave me the chance to meet some of the other young people who would be working there for the summer. I sat down beside Karen W. from Prairie Village, Kansas.

Two more guys joined our tabletop, Mike R. from Claremore and Doug B. from Chickasha, Oklahoma. I let them know I was an Okie and had lived there as a young child. They were being taught to wait tables in the main dining room. I learned the boys' lodging were some small log cabins out back behind the main building. That sounded pleasant enough to me, but then they told me they had to come into the main lodge to shower and shave. With that said, I was pleased I didn't have their quaint housing. The meal was good, and there was even tasty dessert so no complaints in the food department. It was easy for me to overeat. I came from a family of big eaters so I'd have to be careful and not eat too many calories while away from home.

Totally exhausted after cleaning all day in casual clothing, I headed back to my room to rest.

My roommate, Lynn C. from Des Moines, Iowa, had arrived and after getting acquainted with her, we all went to dinner to socialize with everyone else. Overwhelmed by the amount of work I had to do the first day, it left me with little energy to do anything but just sit and listen. Someone mentioned that artist Andy Warhol had been shot that day in his New York City loft and was critically wounded. I wasn't a big fan, but I enjoyed his Pop Art and thought how awful that this had happened to him. As I listened to the details of the shooting, it seemed he was shot by some crazy actress who had just organized a group of women called the "Society for Cutting Up Men."

Although I was all for women's rights, this seemed a little extreme to say the least. But then New York City was in a whole different world out there.

4

After visiting with the kids who I would be working with the rest of the summer, I started feeling better about my strenuous work situation. Going to dinner would actually become the highlight of the workday. I was a social person! As I got ready for bed that evening, I actually looked forward to what the next day would bring. The light by my bedside table was out by 10:00 p.m.

Once the rooms were cleaned the following day, we were to report to the main lobby after lunch to clean and straighten up the sitting area to get it ready for all the people due to arrive on Friday afternoon. As I entered the atrium, everyone was talking about the assassination of New York Senator Robert F. Kennedy at the Ambassador Hotel in Los Angeles, California.

He had just won the nomination for the democratic presidential primary and was shot around midnight. It had only been two short months since the April 4 shooting of Civil Rights leader Dr. Martin Luther King Jr. when he was killed in Memphis, Tennessee at the Lorraine Motel.

The nation was once again shocked with disgust and disbelief. *What is wrong with our country?* I thought. Wasn't it enough that so many of our armed forces, boy soldiers as they were, had been killed daily in Vietnam? This unpopular war that had divided our homeland for too long was devastating enough. How many more tragic deaths had to happen before it all stopped? I was bewildered and saddened for the well-known Kennedy family and their loss of yet another prominent and promising son in the realm of politics.

Our country seemed to be on the verge of a revolution, especially among the younger people.

I had witnessed the unrest on my own college campus before I left for Colorado. Because I lived at home while going to school, I wanted to escape awhile during the summer months and find a change of scenery for myself. This was supposed to be my therapeutic breather, but I couldn't seem to get away from it all. American culture and politics were exploding out of control. More disturbing news of what was happening in our country followed me out here. I was of the same sentiment of the words from the song "Revolution" by John Lennon and Paul McCartney.

A gathering of people sat around the fireplace in the lobby after dinner, singing songs in remembrance to Bobby Kennedy. It was hard to believe he was gone, leaving his wife and eleven children behind. Everyone's moods were rather somber as we sang while accompanied by a few guitar players. Dave N. from Hattiesburg, Mississippi, and Paul G. from Correctionville, Iowa played Bob Dylan's song "Blowing in the Wind", then a Judy Collins folksong, "Both Sides Now," and finally, the popular song from the movie with the same name, "Born Free". It was a fitting tribute to a good man whose life was worth living and was now gone too soon.

I was up bright and early the next morning for more cleaning, and because Lynn was in training, I was told to pair up with Fran from Norman, Oklahoma. I immediately let her know I had been born in Tulsa and had even lived in Muskogee for a while. After work, we decided to go horseback riding. There were stables on the main property for the guests, but the employees could ride if horses were available. The first busloads of tourists were due around dinnertime so we took advantage of a short outing after work despite the cool and rainy weather. It seemed to be cold all the time in this high altitude so we weren't out long. Nevertheless, we galloped our houses on a thrilling ride around the more opened spaces between the hills and valleys of the terrain as well as the dirt trails.

It reminded me of when I was a child growing up in the country outside Springfield. Our family had a couple of ponies named Tony and Spice, and many days were spent with my brothers and my good friends Jana, Mary Ellen, Judy, and Linda on these wild and wooly chargers around the farmyard and in the back fields and wide-open spaces.

In the dining hall that evening, the staff was told by night management we were welcome to mingle in the lobby with the guests to answer any questions they might have as well as play cards and other board games with each other. It was a family owned establishment and the visitors were to be treated as such to make them feel at home. We were also informed there would eventually be an entertainment night for the guests and they wanted us to work up some skits to perform. If anyone had any special talents, they were encouraged to try out for the upcoming evening show. I had taken piano lessons a few years while growing up and could maybe play the duet "Heart and Soul" with someone so I was willing to get involved.

That dreaded day arrived as I got to clean bathrooms after they'd been used by the visitors. It was unpleasant enough to clean up after myself and my family's toilet but scrubbing the commode of someone you didn't know was absolutely gross! I decided right then and there that I hated cleaning bathrooms. Because the Gray Lines busloads of tourists stayed at the lodge for several days, Mrs. Mosley suggested we leave an envelope on their room desk with our names and home state listed in hopes of getting a nice tip when they checked out at the end of the week.

Talk at dinner that evening was the news that James Earl Ray, the man who had shot Dr. Martin Luther King Jr. had been arrested in London and would be sent back to the United States. It would not bring back Dr. King, but his killer was caught and justice would prevail.

In the lobby on Saturday nights was square-dancing, and I went down to watch the couples do-si-do and allemande left and right around the room. Robert W. from Kingsville, Texas and I volunteered to babysit some of the preschool-aged kids while their parents twirled and swung to the promenade caller as the fiddlers played and hooped and hollered. I made a little extra money that night, but at a dollar an hour, it wasn't anything to write home about.

***

Sunday morning came bright and early as eight of us got up to go to the 6:30 a.m. Mass.

I grew up Catholic and attended parochial grade schools, so going to church on Sunday was the norm in my family. There were, in fact, lots of fish eaters working at the chalet for the summer.

This was perhaps, because when submitting your application for the job, you had to have a reference letter from your preacher. The Catholic kids could easily obtain one from their priest as long as they went to church. That Sunday morning, several of the guys had cars so we all crammed into two small vehicles and headed down the hilly, curvy road into the town of Estes Park to attend Mass at Our Lady of the Mountains Catholic church. It was a lovely rock building built in 1949, the year I was born. We planned to get up early every Sunday and go to Mass before work. With most visitors checking out Sundays, we didn't have to report for work till eight o'clock. Then we had a boat load of work to do, getting ready for the next bus load of folks arriving later in the day.

One of the newer girls, Nancy Moore from Wichita, Kansas and I were assigned to work together since Lynn was not feeling well that day. The girls were allowed to wear street clothes to work so jeans and sweatshirts were the cleaning attire. Nancy and I seemed to hit it off, and it was nonstop talking while we worked. She was also smaller in stature and blond like me, but her hair was cut fairly short. Nancy had just finished her second year in college at Kansas State in Manhattan. She wanted to work in Colorado for the summer since her high school squeeze would be working at a resort out here as well.

Although we were still not used to the altitude and seemed to get fatigued much quicker, later in the evening, Nancy and I went into town with some of the other kids to a dance hall called Jax Snax. As we were waiting our turn to enter the nightclub, I noticed lots of hippies hanging around this little town. I was more conservative and "straight laced" as my dad would call me.

Maybe I was more prim and proper and a fashion conformist. Their eccentric lifestyle was not for me, but here in Estes Park, I could witness a subculture you didn't see much of back in the mid-West where I came from. There had actually been a recent article in the local tabloid, the *Estes Park Trail*

Left to right, Gina, Nancy, Dee and Janet

Gazette about a young girl from Iowa who was led astray by a twenty-year-old hippie. The paper described her as living with a mob of other young people who were "dirty, ill-adjusted, and anti-social." But these groovy dressed flower children liked listening to the same music I did as we bopped together, sharing the dance floor and watching each other dance. I could handle the mixed company here, just not in some hippie commune somewhere.

The band played songs by The Beatles and Jim Morrison and The Doors. I preferred more rock-n-roll, but I would dance to just about anything. Now I was getting anxious to write home and tell my family about my new girlfriends and my first week away from home in this thought-provoking place. I'd send the newspaper clipping and tell my dad, despite the distance between us, "he didn't have to worry about his daughter being led astray by some long-haired hippie."

Chapter Two: Monday, June 10

After all the complaints about work, today was so slow they let us off early. With very few guests at the lodge, there wasn't that much to do, and we weren't due for another big group till mid-week. Several of us went into town to do laundry. While waiting on the washers at the local laundromat, we walked around town and checked out some of the shops. There were lots of tourist-trap souvenir stores, and I bought a few postcards, but we mostly just looked at all the junk while waiting for our clothes to dry. I did buy some leather Indian moccasins since the loafers I had brought with me were not practical for work, and I got a pair of khaki-colored jeans that were more comfortable for cleaning on cool days. I honestly thought we'd be provided with uniforms. In my travels, I'd never seen maid-service ladies cleaning in cut-off jeans and t-shirts.

Returning to the lodge, we were greeted by Mr. Davidson, the personnel manager. When I introduced myself as Dee Davidson, he said he remembered reading my application and that was why he approved my hiring. *So that was why?* I thought to myself. It was because of my last name that I got the job and not because of the outstanding reference letter from Father Sullivan.

Nancy and I checked to see if we could work as partners, and Mr. D. agreed to tell Mrs. Mosley.

One of the guys, Ron B. from St. Joseph, Missouri invited us over to his cabin after dinner for a get-acquainted gathering. He was the head bellhop and a tall, nice-looking guy who I enjoyed talking to. Coincidentally, he had just graduated from SMS (my college), but I don't ever remember seeing him. Being older than most of us, he could buy beer, wine, and liquor. I was still trying to develop a taste for alcohol, and it sure wasn't beer. I preferred a sweeter taste than most. Since I wasn't drinking much, I felt uncomfortable and left. Back in my room, I couldn't help but think about Ron. *What a small world*, I thought, *that we were at the same school last year.* Was I feeling a little crush coming on for this older man? I guess as long as members of the opposite sex have shared close quarters, romantic liaisons have been a concern.

The following work day was extremely slow again so we were off early and another trip back to town ensued, this time to buy Father's Day presents. Many of the stores were family owned and operated with handcrafted and one-of-kind unique collectibles. We strolled up and down the street, peeking into many of the windows before finding an affordable gift shop. Luckily, we befriended Gerry M. from Denver because he had a car to provide rides. In fact, Nancy asked him if he would drive to Grand Lake that afternoon to pick up her boyfriend. Stan was a student at Colorado State in Ft. Collins, and he was working at the Grand Lake Lodge for the summer. He had some time off from his job, and we were all off work the next day too.

The drive on Highway 34 through the Kawuneeche Valley was absolutely gorgeous with intoxicating views in every direction. I was getting that Rocky Mountain high from the sights and sounds of the surrounding beauty. Along the streamside were blue spruces intermixed with dense stands of lodge pole pines. Here and there appeared groves of aspen with their noticeable white bark. Wildflowers dotted the meadows and clearings with hundreds of butterflies fluttering around. The sky-colored Colorado columbine is the state flower. Deer, elk, and other wildlife were spotted on the journey. Elk, called wapiti by Native Americans, congregate in open fields, by the side of the highway. Like deer, they are antlered animals. Each year, the bulls shed their bone-like substance that spans five feet and have six points. Closely related to the elk are the mule deer with large wondering eyes and enormous ears. We all laughed at Nancy when she nicknamed them "Mr. Big Ears." Back in Missouri, the whitetail deer were more common.

We picked up Stan at Grand Lake Lodge, which was also operated by Estes Park Chalet, Inc. This mountain paradise was situated near the beautiful lake. Stan loved to fish, and he told us the lakes and streams around were filled with native greenback, cutthroat, rainbow, brown, and brook trout.

I told him I was not a fisherman, but there were lots of bass and catfish at Table Rock Lake near my hometown in Branson. Darkness descended on the way back, and time was consumed with enjoyable conversation. Stan was a delightful fella, tall and blond with thick, black, horn-rimmed glasses. I could see why Nancy adored him as they talked incessantly on the drive back.

***

I had not slept-in since arriving in Estes Park and on my day off it was nice to be lazy.

Nancy was off somewhere with Stan. The better part of the late morning I wrote letters to family and replied to the ones I'd received from friends back home. I missed my best friend Becky; she also applied for a job out here but didn't get hired. I leisurely washed my hair and went outside to let it dry on the first warm day in the mountains. The afternoon was beautiful so I sat out by the pool to soak up the sun rays in the almost eighty degrees temperature. I was cautioned by Barbara, another Denver local; she said I needed to be careful up here in this dry mountain air due to the higher altitude. Evidently because you were closer to the sun, you could get sunburned faster, even though the sun didn't feel as hot. This was good news to me because, if what she was saying were true, then it would only take about half the amount of time to get tanned.

While I was sitting outside, the new tour bus arrived with all the Shriner Conventioneers, and I watched them disembark for their vacation at the chalet. After dinner that evening, I went for a walk with Kent from Iowa. He shared with me that he had experimented with drugs, which I had not, so he rather intrigued me with what he had to say. I'm not sure if he was testing my reaction to see if maybe I wanted to participate or just trying to shock me. Probably many of the kids out here had smoked marijuana, but at this time in my life, I had no desire to partake. The minor hurts and emotional pain in my life had not been traumatic enough to drive me to drink or use drugs. *To each his own!* I thought, on this quiet and tranquil first day off from work. But then again, every day seemed like a holiday day out here. I loved summers, and life didn't get any better!

Nancy and I were up at the crack of dawn, back to the day shift of straightening up the occupied rooms. Working with Nancy could be quite comical. She had a great sense of humor and cracked jokes about everything. The days went faster since we started working together. We left a small envelope with our names and the name of the college we attended in every room we cleaned. The tips started coming, some better than others, but they all added up. Each week we were assigned to different floors and sections of the numerous buildings.

There were more than fifty young people working at the lodge in various capacities over the summer so it was a busy hotel and required lots of cooperation and teamwork. The kids were from both the East Coast and West Coast and numerous states in between. The guys worked as waiters and had to dress in nice white shirts with Western string black bow ties. A few of the guys were bellhops. The girls were maids and front-desk operatives. The cooks and kitchen help and the maintenance were an entirely different department altogether. Nancy and I were a good team. She amused me with her winning personality, and I laughed at all her funny stories.

We made time for Kodak moments and took mindless photos of each other in our room. I had the kind of smile that seemed to attract attention from others even when I wasn't trying to entice. We both felt fortunate to be living and working in this captivating place with such a romantic flair for whatever sparked your interest. I could hardly wait for what was in store ahead for us.

The week seemed to fly by as we continued to explore our surroundings when time allowed us away from our work. Not far from the lodge were some gigantic rocks and Berny C. from New Orleans, Louisiana and I climbed them in the twilight just so we could sit and watch the sunset.

Some of us even walked a little farther up the hill one evening and traipsed through a bit of snow that had not yet melted away. This rugged country had been a National Park since 1915 and an obvious feature of the area is the marked differences found with the changing elevation. At lower levels in the foothills are the ponderosa pine, juniper, and Douglas fir trees. We never stayed out too long after sundown as the temperatures quickly dropped to an uncomfortable shiver.

***

John and Butch, the boyfriends of Gina and Janet, drove out from Missouri for the weekend, which inspired another trip to the infamous Jax dancing establishment for more exercising and tapping of feet to the sounds of Led Zeppelin and B.B. King. I wasn't really a fan of the heavy metal sounds and this particular band was really loud. They also had a psychedelic light show going on with some Janis Joplin songs while we danced. This was as wild and crazy as I dared be, but we were having a pre-celebration gala for my nineteenth birthday, which was the next day. Then they played a song by Sly and The Family Stone, "Dance to the Music," a song I could dance to.

On Sunday, everyone working at the chalet knew June 16 was my birthday. Everyplace I went I was wished happy birthday, even by some of the guests as we worked through the busy morning. In fact, one man told me that golfer Lee Trevino won the U.S. Open in New York so it was a good day to celebrate. Nancy and I made a whole $6.50 in tips that day. There was a bouquet of wildflowers waiting on the dinner table that evening as all the kids broke out in song. After eating, I made a collect call home so I could talk to my parents. Plus, it was Father's Day, a "holiday," and I wanted to wish my dad well. I always loved it when our special June days fell on the same day, and this year I wasn't even there to celebrate with him. As I hung up the phone, it hit me I only had one more year left being a teenager before I had to convert to a "responsible adult."

While trying to go to sleep that night, I kept thinking about my family back in Missouri and the new friends I was making in Colorado. Being the only girl with five brothers, I was used to lots of attention, though not always welcomed. The friendships seemed to form quickly out here, far away from the comforts of familiar faces and relationships. I was probably a tad homesick as I thought about my temporary family and friends at the chalet. I wondered how much of myself I wanted to disclose and the secrets I would share with my newfound friends. There was a part of me that did more listening than talking when it came to certain subjects. We were all still in the process of getting to know each other, and I was being optimistically cautious.

Almost two weeks had passed since my arrival, and I was very much a part of this miniature community. Of course, there were certain individuals who I felt closer to than others, but most everyone here seemed to care about each other as it was so joyfully demonstrated this particular day. All the well wishes I received for my birthday, even some from perfect strangers, was so unexpected. Gerry, one of those Mr. Drama darlings who you would never be infatuated with but you liked him just the same, gave me a turquoise necklace, and I bought a ring to match that I saw in the hotel lobby gift shop. Almost any shade of blue I liked and especially the darker hues.

The native Indians in Colorado made lots of turquoise jewelry so I was thrilled to have some.

There was so much ahead of me to learn about life and my future and this unique place was giving me opportunities I would not otherwise have for discoveries. It was my new mini-dorm experience of living away from home and being on my own without supervision. Although there were some rules and regulations here too, like no boys in the girls' residence area, and we were not allowed to smoke upstairs due to fire hazards. Nicotine was not an addiction of mine so this rule didn't prohibit any of my life practices. But this was a time to test my self-discipline, my morals, and my values away from parental guidance. I wondered how I would perform with no restraints. My thoughts were interrupted by a welcome phone call from Ronnie.

Chapter Three: Monday, June 17

Mondays always seemed to be our busiest days as most folks were checking out, and we were hard at work getting the rooms ready for the next crowd of vacationers. I was glad to see the Masonic Shriners, who were mostly a bunch of drunks, leave. One morning, this man decided to spray us with a squirt gun, and then he picked up our cleaning solutions and proceeded to do the same thing. We tried to make light of it, but I was afraid it would get in my eyes.

Most of the time, we finished by noon since the buses left early and the people were checked out so we could clean. Nancy and I took advantage of the afternoon sun and sat by the pool. Later in the day, we hitchhiked into town to go shopping. I felt fairly safe about hitching rides since there were so many students working in the park for the summer. My older brother Chuck had a June birthday so I wanted to get him a gift. He was away attending his Marine Reserves summer camp in San Diego for a few weeks. When we were growing up, because our birthdays fell within the same week, we usually celebrated together. However, I was a Gemini, the twin personality and the second born so more of a free spirit, craving change and my independence.

His star sign was Cancer, more serious and not as trusting and curious as I was. My younger brother Paul also shared a June birthday. He moved into my bedroom while I was away for the summer and he had just turned sweet sixteen and gotten his driver's license.

***

Tuesdays were usually our slowest days as most of the larger groups of guests did not arrive until Wednesday. Several of us decided to do a small climb up Crag Trail this particular sunny afternoon. Blond-headed David H. from Granite Falls, Minnesota had hiked it and thought we could handle this assent. It was not a technical climb but moderately rated, and we were not required to register, but we left details about our destination with Margaret at the front desk.

Nancy, Gerry, Pam F. from Scottsdale, Arizona, Sue F. from Golden Valley, Minnesota, Richard J. from Champaign, Illinois, Mark C. from Dallas, Texas, Mike R. from Claremore, Oklahoma, and I headed out for the hike up twenty-five hundred feet. I was not properly outfitted since the only shoes I had were my white sneakers. The topography was rough, mostly covered with fallen limbs, sticks, and stones but not many big rocks. Keeping up was a challenge, but we all made it to the top.

Worn-out and almost breathless, I had to lie down on the ground to recover my stamina.

After the break, we sat and ate our box dinners comprised of a ham sandwich, chips, and an apple from the kitchen, which a couple of the guys had carried up in their backpacks. Everyone had to carry their own water or can of pop in their pocket. Different weeds speckled the area, and cute curious chipmunks would pop up from behind logs to see what we were eating. Despite the fact that feeding the rodents was not permitted in the park, I couldn't help but toss a few crumbs their way. When finished, we headed back down the crag, taking our trash with us as there was no dumpster to deposit refuse. We all made it back safely. My first mountain climb was such a rousing adventure, the next purchase I'd have to make would be a pair of hiking boots.

On Tuesday evenings, there was a small group discussion in the community room about faith and religion. One of the employees, Randy F. from Louisville, Kentucky was actually a Baptist youth minister, and he was on his break from the seminary for the summer. He invited all faiths to come and join in the dialogues about our different backgrounds and beliefs. Randy was a big fan of the Reverend Billy Graham, "America's preacher." Although there were no blacks working at the lodge, he welcomed everyone regardless of race, creed or color. It was an enlightening and

educational evening, and I learned some new philosophies. I also found out that Terje V. from Hermosa Beach, California was a Muslim. His parents were from India, and he was a student at Berkeley. I'd never met anyone of the Islamic faith, and it was very informative to hear about his religious customs and convictions. I was trying hard to be more open-minded.

Several of us went out for pizza at Tony's after the meeting and continued our exchanges. I commented that I was disappointed there were no Afro-Americans in our group because I wasn't given the opportunity to get to know many people of color in the town I was raised. I was ready to broaden my perspectives and viewpoints. I wanted to better understand the 'Black Power' movement from someone who walked in those shoes. I'd like to know more about Jesse Jackson, the newest Civil Rights leader who was also an ordained Baptist minister like Dr. King was.

Most evenings Gina or Janet would play one of their albums of relaxing tunes by the San Sebastian Strings. They played other records by top artists like Eric Clapton, Aretha Franklin, and Simon and Garfunkel, but this particular music was by Anita Kerr with words and lyrics by poet, Rod McKuen, "The Sea, The Earth, The Sky". I listened to the calming and soothing sounds of soft ocean waves, cool running water streams, and quiet winds blowing. It was nature's sleep sedative! I would close my eyes and not only hear the restful noises but listen to the unique and gentle voice of Rod McKuen reciting his words of knowledge. One of my favorite songs of his, recently recorded and sung by Bobby Goldsboro, has the following lyrics:

The World I Used to Know

*Someday some old familiar rain will come along and
    know my name.*
*And then my shelter will be gone and I'll have to move
    along.*
*But 'till I do I'll stay awhile and track the hidden coun-
    try of your smile.*

*Someday the man I used to be will come along and call
    on me.*
*And then because I'm just a man, you'll find my feet
    are made of sand.*
*But 'till that time I'll tell you lies and chart the hid-den
    boundaries' of your eyes.*

*Someday the world I used to know will come along and
    bid me go.*
*Then I'll be leaving you behind for love is just a state
    of mind.*
*But 'till that day I'll be your man and love away your
    troubles if I can.*
*And 'till that day I'll be your man and love away your
    troubles if I can.*

Rod McKuen's poetry spoke to just about everyone with messages on life, love, searching, and dying, told in a way that covered every familiar scenario. He was an interesting character who traveled the world, writing along the way about what would later become his famous poems and lyrics. His gift of turning words into verse, limericks, and sonnets would eventually lead him to film composing. Like Rod McKuen, I too loved travel and the sun. Unlike him, I was not gifted in writing prose or rhymes so I just listened.

***

Nancy and I were off on Wednesday, and as hard as I tried to sleep late, all I did was toss and turn so I just got up and wrote letters. I had received several letters from friends so I was trying to get back to them. Because I loved keeping in touch with my many connections, I felt it my obligation to respond to everyone, and I would write to anyone who wrote to me. I'm fairly sure most felt the same as I did. I even wrote to friends of my brothers, Jerry B. and David D. because they wrote to me. Letterhead stationary was provided by the chalet. After Nancy was up and around, we went into town to do laundry before her darling boyfriend arrived.

Stan brought a friend with him, and we all took off for a day trip to Fort Collins to take a tour of Colorado State University where Stan attended. This former United States military outpost from the 1860s is located at the base of the Rocky Mountains. As we walked around the grounds, it became quite clear why Stan liked it here so much. The views were spectacular!

Before heading back to Estes Park, we had dinner at a small café near the college campus.

While driving back, half asleep, and listening to the car radio, the news reported that fifty thousand people had joined in a rally to support the Poor People's Campaign in Washington DC that day with demands of jobs, peace, and freedom. I could not even begin to relate to what they were talking about. The nation's capital seemed light-years away from where we were in the wild, wild west of Colorado. At least it was a peaceful assembly, I pondered, unlike the violent student demonstrations that had happened at Columbia University in New York this past spring. Granted, President Johnson and our government needed to make some drastic changes to the draft and the Vietnam situation, but I hated seeing the violence and property demolition on the television news coverage of the protest marches.

***

Since my arrival, I'd been keeping some late-night hours and still getting up early, so by mid-afternoons, I was dragging my feet. All I wanted to do after work was lounge around in my room or lie out by the pool. This was not like me as I usually had plenty of energy. Not much of a nap taker, I could tell the lack of sufficient sleep was catching up with me. Although my body type only required about six hours slumber each night, I read someplace that a person needed sleep to maintain adequate brain function. I was not getting enough rest to think properly and would have to remedy this situation before losing my mind.

This Thursday night was the first employee talent show in the lobby, and there were several participants who played their guitars and sang popular songs as the onlookers joined in. One of the female staff, who looked like Cher Bono, played an outstanding piano solo. It prompted the management to ask her to play nightly in the restaurant. This casual, impromptu presentation was fun, and Nancy suggested the maids needed to compose a comic routine for the show. She would work on something and solicited our help so we could be ready for the next performance.

After the show, everyone was invited to a barn party near the stables with soft drinks and snacks provided. The fiddlers and a banjo player provided the background music amid the hay bales and straw scattered around the floor. *How exceptional*, I thought, *that the employees are included in the activities planned for the guests*. I wondered if other resorts involved the

23

hired hands with the paying customers in these social settings. This western chalet really was a unique place to work. I was making so many new friends before I really knew them.

The evenings were always cool, it seemed, and you had to wear a jacket after the sun went down. Back in Missouri, you could go swimming at midnight if you felt like it because the temperatures could still be eighty or ninety degrees out. There would not be any of those "hot summer nights" in this mountainous location. We didn't need any air conditioners out here either, and we always had to close the windows in our dorm rooms as evenings approached. It was June, and I was still using a blanket when going to sleep at night.

***

The weekend came and went as Nancy wrote the script for The Chalet Maids routine while Gina, Janet, and I helped out with our input. It was decided we would dress up like the classic hillbilly look of mismatched outfits, rolled-up sleeves and pant legs. Chuckling together, we decided this was pretty much what we looked like every day at work. But we could make our hair disheveled, smear some dirt on our faces, and carry mops and old buckets while singing a song to the familiar tune of "Georgy Girl." The song, written by Tom Springfield and Jim Dale, was made famous by the Australian folk music group, The Seekers. We had all seen the well-known 1966 British movie starring Lynn Redgrave and James Mason. Both were nominated for best actress and best actor respectively. And we were very familiar with the melody of this song that was nominated for an Academy award for Best Original Song from a motion picture.

The following lyrics are what we all wrote together for the song and dance routine talent show.

Chalet maids
Hey there, chalet maids,
Swingin' down the halls with brooms and mops
Workin' every day until we are ready to drop. Chalet maids

Hey there, dusty dames, why do all the waiters pass us by?
Could it be the jeans we wear or is it our stringy hair?
Chalet maids, we're always cleaning toilets and washing
*   sinks all day*
Why don't we ever get time to play? Chalet maids
Hey there sexy slaves, Why don't all the bellhops stop and
*   wave?*
If only we would get more tips, then soon they all would see
That we would be, the new chalet maids.

At dinner we had a little meeting with the other maids who were there and gave them copies of the songs to practice and memorize. The general consensus was favorable, and we decided there would be a rehearsal once everyone learned the words and was able to collect and gather together a costume to wear. The outfits and props would be simple enough to assemble. We were fairly sure Mrs. Mosley would not object to our borrowing some old mops and buckets from the storage closet or anything else we might need.

After dinner that evening, several of us gals went into town to check out another dance place called The Rock, located in The Rock Inn, which was built back in the 1930s. We had heard the band was good and thought it worth our time. This particular group played a blend of country and rock. So, we got to hear a little cowboy mix with songs by Johnny Cash and Glen Campbell and then their rendition of the rock stars, Elvis Presley, James Brown, and others. Sunday night ended with a blast as we girls rocked out with some funky rock at The Rock and with some more blues rock from Fleetwood Mac and Mick Jagger's, The Rolling Stones.

Chapter Four: Monday, June 24

It was change of shift day, and Nancy and I were moved from building north to the first floor south.

The only thing I didn't like about the switch was that we had to clean the public restrooms that were located off the main lobby. That dirty word again, "bathrooms," which I could definitely skip. However, we had to clean the chef's quarters in the other building and this squatty, gruff, former Marine was the biggest slob yet we had to decontaminate. I wasn't sure I ever wanted to eat a meal that he prepared. No doubt the kitchen help probably had to clean up after him too.

There were radios in the guest rooms so we could listen to them while we cleaned. Once in a while, we even danced around the room if so moved. A song I loved to hear was one by Don Fardon called "Indian Reservation", (The Lament of the Cherokee Reservation Indian). As he sang the sad lyrics about the "Trail of Tears" revisited, under the slow-paced melody is a low and rhythmic, constant double-time drumbeat. Every time it came on the radio, I was inspired to do a war dance in my moccasins around the beds. Being from Oklahoma originally, there was a part of me that was sympathetic to the treatment or mistreatment of the Indian tribes.

My hands were broken out with a rash that was probably caused by one of the harsh cleaning products. It was one of the many side effects and hazards of this job that we had to endure. The lodge was expecting a bunch of doctors for a week-long convention, and we were rushing to get the rooms ready for three o'clock check-in. The weather outside was cold and dreary so I withdrew to my room after lunch to write letters home and eat junk food. I get depressed when there's no sunshine to cheer me. We did get our first paycheck so that was something to be joyful about.

I attended the group religion session that evening, which had been rescheduled since the community room would be in use by the doctors on Tuesday. It was incredible to me there were so many different customs, traditions, ethnicities, and behaviors when it came to religious beliefs.

Sometimes the exchange and discussions could get a little heated. It was similar to a religious encounter group of sorts as we were trying to be open and honest about our thoughts and feelings. I'd read about a group of Catholic nuns in California who'd embraced this process of expressing one's true feelings, and it had created some changes in the church. Living a sheltered life, growing up in the Protestant Baptist Bible Belt of southern Missouri left me unaware of some philosophies. At least I'd been exposed to Catholicism or I'd really be ignorant. My parents were converts so I got most of my basic early religious instruction and ideologies while attending Catholic grade schools. Although I did think some of these kids out here were a little on the strange side, I fully intended to take a religion class next semester as one of my college electives to broaden my knowledge and viewpoints on the subject.

On Tuesday morning, those paychecks had to be cashed so Nancy and I hitched into town after work to do a little Christmas shopping. There were restaurants galore with everything from fast-food to trendy cuisine and fine dining. We splurged and went out to eat where I overate so as not to waste any food. Like most kids I knew, when we were young, we were told to clean our plates for all those starving kids in China. I'm not sure how it helped those kids, but you didn't question your parents and now it was hard for me to stop eating until all the food on my plate was gone.

Besides, wasn't it sinful to waste food? I probably had an eating disorder because of all this.

***

I was feeling out of sorts this day, so much so that I was not relaxed with all the doctors everywhere. They were creepy, and

I was almost paranoid that they were making some sort of diagnosis about my health. Unlike the Shriners, who were friendly and talkative, these men were serious and never smiled. They must have been physicians who dealt with life-threatening diseases because they were sure not jubilant like pediatricians and family practitioners. I retired to my room after work to be alone. Although I was off the next day, it must have been that time of the month because I didn't feel good and all I wanted to do was go to bed early.

Thursday was a new day, and I felt rested and ready for a road trip. Nancy had invited me to join her and Stan for a drive to Boulder to see Colorado University. Much like Ft. Collins, the campus was surrounded by mountains and the views were absolutely stunning. I could never get enough of the mountain scenery. In every direction there was a different shaped peak to witness.

There were in fact, 113 named mountains in Rocky Mountain National Park. After having lunch in Boulder, we drove on to the University of Denver to see their facility. I recalled just a few months prior, this private university was in the news when their chancellor, Maurice Mitchell, refused the demands of several students, which resulted in a sit-in on one of the non-public buildings when over forty students were told to either leave or face dismissal. There was no tolerance for the troublemakers, and most were arrested and dismissed from school.

As much as I would love to go to school out here in this beautiful state, my dad would always remind me he had six kids to put through college and going away or out of state was out of the equation. It was a nice muse! To appease myself, I bought a pair of leather Jesus sandals at a local apparel shop before we headed back up to Estes Park for the evening. The Chalet Maids were not ready for their performance so it was decided to postpone our production another week. I opted to babysit for an adorable little Japanese girl named Yuki. After the talent show, we all went to the weekly barn party. Ron was there and we got to talk and socialize. It was a better day!

***

The doctors left on Friday, making it the longest work day we'd had so far. I was glad to see them go, but I will have to say, the tips were well worth their stay. We had to get all the rooms cleaned today because there was another big conference coming in at 5:00 p.m. Nancy was not feeling good so she didn't go back to work after lunch. *Maybe there is a bug going around*, I thought, *with her being sick*. One of the new girls, Nyla T. from Carlos, Minnesota was assigned to work with me. She was in training, but Mrs. Mosley trusted me to coach her while we worked together. What a day! We were certainly ready for a dinner break, but we heard some upsetting news; one of the employees had been let go and would be leaving.

Friday night was Movie Night in the lobby for those who were interested. The films were on reels shown by a projector on the large white wall in the back of the room. If you missed the Friday night showing, it played again on Sunday evening. The movie playing, *Davy Crockett, King of the Wild Frontier,* staring Fess Parker and Buddy Ebsen, most of us had seen when we were in grade school. I thought about watching it again on Sunday night.

Some of the guys went out back and started a bonfire and invited everyone out to sit around the inferno. Dave, the head waiter, played his guitar and we sang the "Hammer Song", made popular by folk singers, Peter, Paul & Mary and "Kumbayah" recently brought back by Joan Baez. Then they played some cowboy tunes as we sang along, "Tumbling Tumbleweeds" and "Cool Water," which were made famous by the western singers Sons of the Pioneers, and we heard a new one just out by Neil Diamond, "Sweet Caroline." As I sat holding myself in the cool evening breeze, I gazed up at the sky and couldn't believe how bright the stars were with no city lights to dim our views. The sounds of the winds gusting through the pine trees added to the dazzling night. WOW! Was all I couldn't stop saying to myself.

***

My dirt partner in crime was still not back to her usual self so Nyla and I paired up again together for dusting duty. Getting off early again, I headed out to sit by the pool for thirty minutes of vitamin D. My skin was getting browner by the day but not getting burned by the "closer sun." After dinner, Nancy was back to her perky self, even a little on the feisty side. She wanted to hang some posters and pictures on the walls in our dorm room. After confiscating some *Playboy* magazine foldouts from Stan the last time we had been together, she hung up some very pretty women who, though not totally nude, "there wasn't much left for the imagination," as my mother would say.

Then Nancy went down the hall, visiting all the girls' rooms and inviting them to come to my abode and view the latest wall hangings. It definitely spruced up the place and added some conversation pieces to the drab interior dwelling. Everyone that came over for the art exhibition got their photo taken standing next to Hugh Hefner's June playmate of the month. Speaking of which, *Time* magazine said last month that Mr. Hefner shared his Chicago mansion with twenty-four girlfriends. Really? He certainly made a fortune off legally exploiting women. But then again, another way of looking at it, as producer Mel Brooks would say, "When you got it, flaunt it."

The 'quartette' or suitemates in room one at the top of the stairs, were properly familiar now with our weekly work routine and of going to Mass on Sunday mornings, then back to the chalet to clean the vacant rooms, preparing for the next group to arrive who'd grace us with their faces.

Janet, Gina, Lynn, and I were becoming more than just dorm mates but friends as well.

Sunday could also be letter-writing day to family and friends back home. I answered letters that day to Marshall D., Jim S., Diane M., Steve B., and two of my brothers. Writing letters was so common with most of us that setting time aside for this important task was a mutual undertaking.

We seldom made phone calls home just to chit-chat due to the inflated expense of long-distance communication. The cost of six cent postage stamps on cards and messages were how we kept in touch as money was never in abundance. My mom had even sent me some stamps in her last letter.

She was also good about sending me articles from our hometown paper of newsworthy updates that I would be interested in knowing. I especially enjoyed the society page with marriage engagement notices, wedding photos, new birth announcements, and police stops.

This particular Sunday evening, Nancy and I decided to get all dressed up and go into town to dance at The Rock. We couldn't talk anyone into going with us, which was probably a good thing, because unbeknownst to either of us, there was a cover charge that night. Between the two of us, neither one of us had enough to pay the entrance fee, and we were turned away. There were other pubs and nightclubs, but we had our heart set on the contemporary rock music joint.

So much for getting all dressed up for nothing, I thought. I had even washed my hair before going out, sitting under that hot portable hair dryer with rollers for almost an hour.

Irritated by all this, we headed back to the chalet and managed to catch a ride with one of the employees who had a car. Valerie W. was from my hometown and we went to Glendale High School together. She worked for the Chalet Inc. at a store located on the Roof of the Rockies at the top of Trail Ridge Road, one of the great alpine highways in the country. It crosses the park from east to west and is the highest continuous paved road in the nation. The roads winding course, with no guardrails by the way, takes you up to over 12,000 feet above sea level, crossing through the Continental Divide and into a world similar to the Earth's arctic regions. According to Valerie, there was still a lot of snow where she worked, and she invited us to come up when we had time to see the Trail Ridge Store that sold food, gifts, and mementoes.

There were actually several girls from Springfield who I knew who were working out here for the summer. Glenda B., Stephanie D., Cathy C., and Linda H. all had jobs at the historic, white-painted Stanley Hotel, just outside the town of Estes Park. This grand Colonial Revival style of architecture inn was built for the American upper class in 1909 by famed Freelan Oscar Stanley.

He invented the Stanley Steamer, or the steam-powered car. Mr. Stanley was directly responsible for the growth of Estes Park into the resort town that it grew to be. Initially, he came to Colorado in the summer of 1903 for health reasons, but his love for the mountains and the beauty of the valley brought him back every year. The rugged and rough territory was mainly used for fishing in the Big Thompson River and hunting big game animals, including elk, moose, and bear until the Rocky Mountain National Park was established in 1915.

Although the original Stanley Manor only had forty-eight rooms, it featured duel electric and gas lighting, a hydraulic elevator, a telephone in each of the rooms, and running water supplied by the Black Canyon Creek. With the railroad station only twenty miles from town, the wealthy patrons were able to travel in a luxury Pullman. They were picked up from the station and transported to the hotel in Mountain Wagons. There was no heat so the Stanley closed down in the winters.

Consequently, Estes Park has never attracted off-season visitors and mainly caters to the summer tourists. However, there is a small secluded ski area at the top of Trail Ridge Road called Hidden Valley that was built in the 1950s.

Today the Stanley Hotel has 140 rooms and still a magnificent structure to visit. Also, in the hotel structure is the F.O. and Flora Stanley Steam Car Museum. Some of us kids decided to drive by one afternoon when we were in town to visit this renowned residence, and we stopped to take a quick tour of the exhibition of old cars. The Stanley Motor Carriage Company was the American manufacturer of steam-engine vehicles called Stanley Steamers, and there were several different models on display.

On occasion I got to see my friends who worked at the Stanley Hotel as waitresses. We'd run into each other in town when out and about shopping or dancing. However, I doubt they got to dress as comfortable as the chalet maids did at this lodge built for middle-class America in 1913.

In fact, the conditions at the Stanley for their employees were not as good as we had it at the chalet and my friends ended up going back to Missouri before the end of summer.

Chapter Five: Monday, July 1

The month of June seemed to fly by but not fast enough to miss adding a few pounds to my waistline. Nancy and I both had been eating too much so we vowed to start cutting back on the sweets in July. We did make a total of $41.00 in tips last month that we split, and after a trip to the laundry mat after work, I bought my waffle-stomper, gray hiking boots. Then we joined a group of kids who wanted to take box dinners and go on a picnic to Bear Lake. It wasn't far from the chalet, and we had heard it was lovely. Actually, on Monday evenings in the lobby, there was a slide show about the local activities and what there was to see and do in the park. This lake was featured as one of the "must see" sites. Although it took an hour to walk up to where the lake was located at over nine thousand feet, it was indescribably beautiful. Considered an alpine snow melt, it was formed during the ice age by a glacier. As you can imagine, the water temperature was freezing. There was still snow on both sides of the lake. The one thing I missed about Missouri was the warm water lakes. I would probably not be doing any water skiing out here this summer. Nine miles away from Bear Lake was an incredible view of Longs Peak, the highest of the parks fourteener mountaintops, which means it is over fourteen thousand feet up.

Several of us hardy souls decided we would climb that summit before leaving Colorado.

To break the monotony of daily cleaning and waiting tables, several times during the week a group of us would go to Jax Snax or The Rock to dance. Well, it was bound to happen sooner or later, as the summer got busier with more and more people visiting the park. I got carded and caught in the act for being under age. The Rock served beer and you had to be twenty-one to get in. One of the chalet guys said it was an easy fix to change the 1949 year on my driver's license to 1947.

So back at the chalet, I gave him my cardboard identification, and he took a razor blade and carefully scratched away the top of the nine so it would look like a seven. I had just gotten a new card after my birthday so I let him alter my old ID card to use while I was away from home. It didn't work as well if you were born in 1948 but so far, Nancy hadn't got carded.

For a while, it felt like we were living in a monsoon season. I actually got caught in a terrible downpour coming in after taking the trash out one day in the back alleyway. You could almost bet on it to rain everyday around two in the afternoon. So instead of sitting out by the pool, I wrote letters to my friends that I had heard from this past week. Debby A. and Becky, my high school pals, and Meri S. and Carole B., my college buds, got to hear all about what was going on in my life on the mountain. There was always someone from my large, extended family that I had to answer back. Even my granddad Frank wrote to me. He would type his letters with lots of errors, but I loved hearing from him about life on the farm with all the news of the barn animals and the vegetable garden. My dad was just like his dad and would type me similar letters about his many summer tasks, tending to blackberries and tomatoes on the Cherry Street acreage.

Here it was, the day before the Fourth of July and rain was predicted. Some of us wanted to have another campfire night out, but the ground was so wet, we ended up going to Ron's cabin and listened to records instead. Ron had had a few too many drinks and he started talking to me and told me he was not looking to get married and I didn't need to have a relationship with him if I was wanting to find a husband. Well, this was news to me as I had a few more years of school yet to complete before I would be ready for marriage. I know I came off as a "nice girl" and didn't mean to give him the wrong impression, but he was certainly jumping to conclusions about us.

Besides, I had several suitors back in Missouri and I had even received a letter from Ronnie that day.

***

On our country's birthday, it looked like the rain would dampen the fireworks show. However, the Thursday night talent show was on schedule. After work, the Chalet Maids rehearsed their skit in the community room to present for the first time. We were a bit nervous but knew the songs and felt prepared. Gina suggested after singing "Chalet Maids" we sing "Consider Yourself" from the Broadway Musical, *Oliver Twist* by Charles Dickens. The movie version *Oliver* was due for release in the fall. We all thought it was a great idea and would be a perfect welcoming greeting to the guests for their stay at the family friendly Estes Park Chalet. Our performance was well received, and we got lots of laughs and applause from the guests and the employees.

The following are the words of the other song we would also sing at the talent performance.

"Consider Yourself"

Consider yourself at home. Consider yourself one of the family.
We've taken to you so strong. It's clear; we're, going to get along.
Consider yourself well in, Consider yourself part of the furniture.
There isn't a lot to spare. Who cares? Whatever we've got we share!
If it should chance to be we should see some harder days.
Empty larder days Why grouse?
Always a chance we'll meet somebody to foot the bill.
Then the drinks are on the house!
Consider yourself our mate. We don't want to have no fuss,
For after some consideration, we can state....
Consider yourself, One of us!

When the show concluded, in the misty rain, we headed out to the red-white-and-blue–decorated barn for the weekly party. The cooks had prepared a patriotic birthday cake and cookies with red, white, and blue frosting. There was even red punch to drink as well as soda pop.

Everyone had a good time despite the fireworks display being cancelled. Since a number of chalet guests came to the celebration, it was too crowded for the employees to stay so most of us left early. The lobby was empty, and we sat by the fireplace and talked while watching the flames from the burning wood. In the background, I could hear one of my much-loved songs playing on the radio, "This Guy's in Love with You," by Herb Alpert and the Tijuana Brass.

The day after the Fourth was another gloomy, hazy day, and most of the guests and employees just hung out at the lodge all day. This particular group would be checking out on Saturday so Friday was an easy day for the maids, and we could rest up for the busy day ahead. At dinner, Mrs. Maps, the dining room hostess, told the maids they could eat for free on Saturday night at the chalet dining room buffet since most of the guests would be checking out, and they expected it to be slow for customers. Several of us decided we'd dress up for our dinner outing in the main dining room.

It was Friday night at the movies, and because it was so nasty rainy and cold out, instead of going into town, Nancy and I stayed in and watched the *The Odd Couple* starring Jack Lemmon and Walter Matthau, originally produced for Broadway. The 1968 comedy was written by Neil Simon who was nominated for an Academy award for Best Adapted Screenplay. This story of two divorced men, who decide to live together even though their personalities are critically incompatible, was actually very funny. One guy was the neat and tidy type while the other guy a fun-loving slob. I'd never seen it before so I was glad I got to see the film for free. There could be advantages of staying in and not spending money, I decided.

Thank goodness we had a restful Friday because Saturday was the busiest day we had had all summer. Nancy and I worked through lunch to try and get everything done, but it was not to our benefit because then we were told to go help the other girls who had not yet completed their rooms. To make matters worse, I stubbed my toe on one of the tables so I was limping around. It was beautiful outside, sunny and warm, and I wanted to get out for some rays. The sun was my friend, and I was happy to see her out again. The only redeeming compensation for this day was all the tips we made after the successful Thursday night show. Mr. Davidson liked it so much he decided he wanted us to perform on Tuesday nights as well. He offered to pay each of us one dollar every time we put on a performance. Anything for a buck! I laughed. After work, I had time for a short swim before getting dressed up for dinner with the girls' night out.

One of the visitors had left an almost full bottle of champagne in their room so we took it back to the dorm and invited some of the other maidens to come by for a toast before we headed down to the banquet meal. Jeannette D. from Houston, TX, Lois B. from Coon Rapids, MN, Sharon D. from Leeton, MO, and Kay M. from Salem, IL raised their glasses with Gina, Janet, Nancy, and me to new friends in old places. Sharon also mentioned her good friend Charla, from Leeton, had a birthday next week so we raised our glasses again to cheer her. The dinner buffet was a wonderful smorgasbord with every kind of dish imaginable. We could choose from roast beef, baked chicken, broiled pork chops, or Rocky Mountain trout with either baked potatoes or mashed potatoes, tossed salad, Jell-O fruit cups or soup du jour. The dessert table was a yummy assortment of different kinds of fruit tarts, Boston cake pie, and various ices or sherbets. I ate till I was stuffed and went back to my room to collapse on my bed.

I could hardly get out of bed Sunday morning to make the early Mass so I told the girls I would go to the 7:00 p.m. evening service. The Catholic church makes it impossible to skip Mass on Sunday because they give you a variety of different times to choose from. There's Saturday evening, early morning on Sunday, late morning on Sunday, and Sunday evening, whatever suits you. I personally like late Sunday morning so I can leisurely get ready without rushing around like I have to all the other mornings of the week. So, I had another choice that I would take that day. In fact, I decided I wanted to do this the rest of the summer. I am not a morning person!

Before getting ready for church after work, I went for a short hike with Jan T. from Rockville, Maryland and got to try out my new boots. They certainly were much better for climbing over rocks than my Keds canvas tennis shoes. We sat on a large rock to gaze at the mountain views at dusk while talking about how lucky we were to be out here in this simply marvelous park. The sky was amazing with all the different colors and shades of reds, oranges, and pinks splattered across the glowing but cloudy sky. It truly was America the beautiful! I was worshiping outdoors in the wilderness, as I could feel the presence of God while surrounded by the glorious purple mountain majesties. The hike ended as we headed back to get ready for indoor church.

When I got back to the dorm after Mass, I read some of Rod McKuen's poems and songs that were written on the booklet inside Gina's record album. I started furiously copying down his words in the back of my journal. Some of his messages were amusing and witty, and others were gloomy and depressing, but most of them enlightening. Somehow his lyrics were helping me sort through my own feelings about life's purpose and meaning. After an hour or so, I got tired of writing and decided I would purchase the album myself so I could have them in my possession. I thanked Gina for introducing me to this wonderful man and all his songs and poems that I loved.

We talked about his influence and how his words were a source of comfort to so many out there.

Janet came in after a trip into town and interrupted our conversation. She'd heard on the car radio that Abbie Hoffman announced "The Yippies are going to Chicago" for the Democratic National Convention in August. The Yippie, a hippie who had been mugged by politics, had been in the news quite often lately. We continued talking about Abbie Hoffman and Jerry Rubin, the founders of the Youth International Party. These pot-smoking peaceful marchers against the war in Vietnam were not common in the US until recent years. Like most everyone, I was ready for the war to be over, but I was surprised anyone listened to these guys since they were over thirty. The Yippie's were following new pursuits and it would be interesting to see what happened in August. It was getting late, and we were all ready to turn out the lights for the night.

Chapter Six Monday, July 8

Many mornings I would not get up in time for breakfast before reporting to work. It forced Nancy and me to steal sweet rolls off the bread truck that drove up to the service entrance each day. They were not the most nutritious food for a diet, but it held us over till lunchtime. The next time we went to town, I bought some fruit for my room to eat instead of the fatty starches. There was a Watermelon Feed at the chalet to welcome the new group of guests, and the employees were asked to attend and help out. It was nothing more than passing out the melon slices to everyone. There sure were lots of activities that revolved around food, making it difficult to control my weight. Food seemed to be my remedy for dealing with life's frustrations and anxieties. I needed to find another cure to comfort my concerns.

Regardless of what I thought about Ron, he continued to be a source of ambiguity in my life.

He invited Nancy and me to dinner with him and his friend Cliff and then he wanted to check out a dance place called the Dark Horse Bar. Despite my apprehension, we went out and enjoyed the strobe-light show that was part of the entertainment in the Riverside Ballroom, next to the tavern.

Dancing the night away to a tune by Tommy James and the Shondells called "Mony Mony" and a new one by The Doors called "Hello, I love You." It was another evening out after midnight as we closed the place down.

***

There was a full moon out, and several of us in the different work teams wanted to camp out overnight. After dinner Berny,

Dave, Greg, Kay, Rick, Nancy, and I gathered up minimal gear, which consisted of a sleeping bag and some water to drink. No snacks were allowed because they would draw bears. Then we took a very short walk not far from the lodge to an area that was surrounded by pine trees and large boulder rocks. We gathered small rocks to form a fire pit circle, and then we collected some dry sticks and tree limbs to build that fire. It was almost dark as the blaze started to mature with the snap, crackle, and pop of burning wood. I threw in a few pinecones, creating that familiar smell of Christmas.

While sitting in the ambiance of nature's great outdoors, we talked and told stories for several hours. There were occasional rustling noises when the wind blew through the trees. Dave picked up his guitar and attempted to play a new song by The Rascals called "People Got to Be Free." *How appropriate*, I thought, *it doesn't get much freer than being out here camping.* As the embers and sparks of the fire started to die down, I snuggled up in my sleeping bag and tried to go to sleep. I watched to make sure the flames were almost out; we didn't need a visit from Smokey Bear. Sleeping through most of the night, the few times I did wake up, I opened my eyes and looked at the pretty stars and fell back to sleep. Most of us were up with the sunrise and walked back to the chalet for a hearty meal. This very early morning I made it to breakfast!

Being off for the day, I leisurely got ready to enjoy my play. Swiping an empty wooden Coke case in the back alley of the lodge, I decided to paint it green and use it for storing some of my many treasures. I had gradually accumulated some things that I'd bought while living here the past month, and I needed a place to put them. There was my Rocky Mountain National Park souvenir glass mug and my new jewelry. Plus, I'd picked up some unusual rocks and colorful stones that I wanted to display. My grandmother, who we fondly called Wimpy, once told me, "You should surround yourself with what makes you happy," and that was what I planned to do with my stuff.

Later in the evening, a group of us went into town and found a peaceful coffee house with a single guitar player sing-

ing some ballads and folksongs. The atmosphere was quieter than the usual loud dance places so we could have a meaningful conversation and be heard. The quiet discussions began with one of the guys mentioning that President Lyndon Johnson and others had signed a Treaty on the Non-Proliferation of Nuclear Weapons. I wasn't sure what all that meant, but it sounded kind of scary. Someone else stated that Saddam Hussein was rising to power in Iraq as the Baath Party revolution continued. And here we all were in beautiful Colorado just living our lives as usual, and yet the nation seemed to be riddled with trouble. I was just happy for tennis star Billie Jean King for winning again at London's Wimbledon in women's singles this past week. I'd taken more of an interest in tennis since my dad had become a tennis enthusiast.

Nonetheless, it seemed we could never have any serious dialog without talking about Vietnam.

The unending protests in opposition to the war had continued in various parts of our country as well as abroad. Although the US had had a small presence in the war effort since 1950, they had escalated their involvement in 1960 and had continued to increase our troops there to such a degree that it didn't make much military logic anymore. Almost twenty thousand of our young men had died, and we all agreed it was time for the killing over there to stop. Even the song we were listening to in the background, which was John Denver's "Leaving on a Jet Plane" could be interpreted as a soldier going off to Vietnam. There was also a new movie out about Vietnam starring John Wayne called *Green Berets* that everyone wanted to see.

***

Nancy wanted to get the maids together on Thursday for a talent show practice. We needed a little polishing up with the routine and going over the songs. Although there were no solo acts, the group as a whole needed some improvement for tonight's performance. It was easy to get everyone collected before or after dinner since we all ate together and lived down the hallway from each other. One of the gals suggested we sing the "Mickey Mouse March" as we exited the lobby. Nancy noted it was like getting a 'Minnie Mouse Club' organized with all the chatter of a dozen females talking at once. We added the following song to the maids' departing exodus.
Chalet Maids March:

Who's the Leader of the Club
That's made for you and me
C-H- A- L- E- T- M- A- I- D- S
Hey there, hi there, ho there
You're as welcome as can be
C- H- A- L- E- T- M- A- I- D- S
Chalet Maids
(Chalet Guests)
Chalet Maids
(Chalet Guests)
Forever let us hold our buckets high
(High high high)

Come along and sing the song
And join the jamboree
C- H- A- L- E- T- M- A- I- D- S
Chalet Maids Club, Chalet Maids Club
We'll have fun, we'll meet new faces
We'll do things and we'll go places
All around the room we're marching
Yeah Maids, yeah Maids
Yeah Chalet Maids Club Yeah

Due to the large crowd of folks at the show that evening, Mr. Davidson had all the kids who contributed come back up and introduce themselves and tell what state we were from. Then he had us sing the first verse of "Happy Trails," which we all knew from watching the Roy Rogers and Dale Evans TV programs growing up in the fifties. It was a perfect ending!

***

Letting the tourist groups know more about who was cleaning their rooms did seem to help with additional tips. Some of the guests even wrote little notes to us, complementing our talents and thanking us for the entertainment. It was our beloved, housekeeping manager's birthday so at dinner, we had a surprise cake and well wishes for her. She was a kind and empathetic boss, who we all appreciated, making it easy to do something special for her.

Greg, one of the kind, good-looking stable hands asked me to watch the Friday night movie *Wait Until Dark*. This suspenseful thriller about a blind housewife starred one of my favorite actresses. I had loved Audrey Hepburn, the beautiful film and fashion icon, since seeing her in the 1964 musical *My Fair Lady*, which had won eight Academy awards, including Best Picture, and the Best Actor award went to Rex Harrison. Although the British starlet didn't win any nominations, she won a place in the hearts of many in this country. She was truly 'loverly!'

The weekend was very busy with one big group checking out and another big group checking in. The maids helped

45

each other, assisting on the other floors, if needed, to finish-up cleaning.

Several million people visited Rocky Mountain National Park each year, and I think half of them stayed with us at the chalet. When it was so hectic, it made it hard to get outside and enjoy the weather till late in the day. But I guess that's why they call work "work." No time for the weary.

Several of us gals decided to take a box lunch out back and sit with nature and immerse with the sunbeams. Mary's Lake was well within our picnic viewing as we munched on crackers. A natural water basin, it was surrounded by dramatic rock outcrops and scrub growth. We learned from the history of the area that over a hundred years ago the Arapaho Indians survived around the lake. There were battles with the Apaches and Utes over hunting rights to the bighorn sheep in the vicinity. While eating my baloney sandwich, I tried to imagine the Indians in their tepees.

I received a long letter from home about what was going on back in Missouri. My mom let me know she missed me since she had to do the ironing that I usually did. Between all my dad's white shirts he wore to work every day as a traveling salesman and my five brother's shirts, sometimes I would iron fifty shirts on a Saturday morning. I sure didn't miss the ironing, as I chuckled to myself. Some of the girls here ironed the waiters' shirts, but I was happy to take the summer off from sprinkling water out of a pop bottle on the winkled material before pressing the cotton tops. Mom also let me know that some of my friends, Debby, Arnie, Billie, and John had been in car accidents, but no one was seriously injured. I cherished the news about my family and friends and the newspaper clippings she included as well.

The large group of mackerel-snappers left for Sunday night Mass after dinner. Afterward, we walked around town and stopped at the grand opening of the new Munchin House, old-fashioned, homemade ice cream shop. They had a variety of different flavors, but I just got a plain vanilla cone. My parents didn't have chocolate candy in the house when I was growing up so I wasn't addicted. It was a well-deserved treat for our over-worked bodies. Back at the chalet, Sunday night at the movies started before ending the week. We got to see the last showing of Andy Griffith's TV series that had recently ended after eight seasons. I always enjoyed watching this comedy about Andy, the widowed sheriff in the small fictional town of Mayberry. I never cared much for his deputy Barney Fife, played by Don Knotts, but his young son Opie, played by cute little Ron Howard, stole the hearts of everyone with his precocious remarks.

Chapter Seven: Monday, July 15

Nancy and I were floaters this week with no assigned floor but filling in for those maids who had days off. It was a pleasant change of pace, working new areas every day, but it also meant we would not get any tips at the end of the week. We were done after lunch and needed to go into town to do laundry along with everyone else at the chalet who had run out of clean clothes for the week. While walking around town, waiting on the washing machines, I ran into Donna B.,one of my high school sorority sisters from Springfield. *What an unbelievable, chance meeting*, I thought as we visited about being in Colorado.

Tuesday, we worked the pool unit, cleaning the rooms closest to the swimming pool. At lunch, there was some gossip going around about one of the horse handlers running off with the bar maid. I'm sure they were both of age, but it was still something to talk about at the meal tables.

Then there was an announcement that if anyone wanted to make some extra money, we could help serve food at the Lazy B Ranch chuck wagon supper that evening not far from the chalet.

Nancy and I and some others decided we would go and see what this entailed.

The Lazy B Ranch served an authentic cowboy dinner including bar-b-que beef, baked beans, corn on the cob, buttered, homemade biscuits, and blackberry cobbler. We got to eat before the supper began, and then we served, cafeteria style, with big metal spoons from large baking pans filled with the food. Hungry guests ate on aluminum plates in an old barn filled with rows of long tables covered with red and white gingham tablecloths. The visitors helped themselves to iced tea or lemonade served in tin cups. While eating, they were entertained with a country western comedy show. I especially enjoyed the banjo player and will never forget when the announcer introduced him, telling the audience to be sure and watch his fingers because they never left his hand while he played his instrument. After the western dinner show, we all headed back to the chalet to perform in the Tuesday night lobby, employee-show production.

***

Valerie had driven down to the chalet for some supplies, and we decided to ride back up with her to see the Trail Ridge Store on our day off. The drive up was a scenic tour with far-spreading views of stunning sites. We stopped at one of the overlooks to take in the Rocky Mountain's peaks and valleys. Along the upper edges of the subalpine ecosystem, the trees are twisted and grotesque and appear to hug the ground. Further up the road, we saw vistas of glacier-carved points on every side. Just as Valerie had told us before, there was still a lot of snow, and even some fearless skiers were taking their chances on a few runs through the rough summer thaw. It was a little chilly up there at 12,000 feet so I was happy to go inside the store to buy postcards and eat a bite in the coffee bar. The entire Trail Ridge Road is fifty miles, but we just went to the store and back, catching a ride down with another employee. On the way down, I noticed the dark forests of Engelmann spruce and an opening where there were wildflower gardens of rare beauty.

Several kids wanted to go see a movie after dinner. Although I'd already seen *The Graduate*, that was the flick that was playing at the local cinema in town so along with my new friends, I watched this show again starring Dustin Hoffman and Katherine Ross. The story was about a twenty-one-year-old recent college graduate with no aim as to what he was going to do in life. I hoped by the time I got out of college, I would know what to do with my life. It was actually a good romantic comedy-drama so I didn't mind going along with the crowd. On the way back to the chalet, the car radio reported that Saddam Hussein had become the president of Iraq that day. Then that news was interrupted by a flat tire and that was all I heard. Everyone got out of the car while the problem was fixed and eventually we got back to the chalet and to bed after midnight.

***

Thursday was an exceptionally busy day working the north wing with a full house. There had been a big party bash in one of the rooms the previous night and shaving cream had been sprayed all over the walls with eighteen beer cans lining the windowsill. Needless to say, we had some extra scrubbing to do. Then Nancy and I both smashed our fingers folding up a rollaway bed, and to add insult to injury, I caught my dirty linens bag on the fire extinguisher hanging in the hallway, knocking it down, as I watched it spray the contents all over the walls and carpet. We certainly did not have time for all these shenanigans as we had the talent show to present that evening.

On a lighter note, it was Ron's birthday so I made him a birthday card after work, and my silly friend Nancy thought it would be funny to wrap up a pair of bikini panties and include it as a gift from the Chalet Maids. It would keep him guessing as to whom they belonged. Several of us were by the pool after work, and I asked Paul, Ron's good pal, to get him to come out so we could give him his special present. He loved his "itsy bitsy teenie weenie" surprise.

Friday continued to be busy with a weekend meeting of some IBM employees (International Business Machines Corporation) and their families staying at the chalet for three days. It was one of the largest groups we had had so far. Nancy and I were working for Janet and Gina and my devious-minded companion added to one of the maid's notes, "cleaned by the handicapped."

I hoped for their sake it would make them a bigger tip. Later that afternoon, we helped out in the chalet nursery. There were numerous little toddlers running around. Definitely ready for a break before dinner, I relaxed in my room to read amusing let-

ters from my special guy, Mike W., and my more than special granddad. In colorful detail, I got to hear all about the upgrading of the fence my seventy-five-year-old grandfather was in the process of reconstructing. He also informed me he had quit smoking cigarettes but did on occasion light up his pipe. This was good news! Mike's letter made my heart smile with his silly tales and stories of what was going on in his life.

Later that evening, a couple of employees from The Elkhorn Lodge came by in an old pick-up truck to see if anyone wanted to go to Lake Estes Drive-In movie theater. *Bonnie and Clyde* was showing, so fourteen of us piled in the cab and the bed of the truck and headed out to see the show starring Faye Dunaway and Warren Beatty. This biographical gangster film was the true story about a young couple during the Great Depression who went from small-time holdups to big-time bank robberies. Eventually, their offenses escalated into violence, killings, and their own demise when they were gunned down by the police after a long crime spree. Before the show started, there was a preview of a Beatles film opening that week called *Yellow Submarine.*

Although I loved the Beatles English rock band music, this children's animated musical comedy didn't look like something I cared to see. British fantasy was not my "cup of tea."

Even though July is one of the warm months for the short Colorado summers, the evenings could still get cool. There were some old blankets in the truck that we wrapped up in while watching the outdoor cinema. Several guys even bought some popcorn that we shared. Driving back to the lodge offered an exceptional opportunity to see another spectacle of shooting stars in the beautiful nighttime, north central Colorado skies. This place never ceased to amaze me with its fascination and attractions. Oh, how I would miss the mountains when I had to go back to Missouri. My life would never be the same in more ways than one.

***

I didn't sleep very well after a late night out so I got up before breakfast and went outside to pick up some pinecones that I wanted to use for room decorations. Work was slow going, and naturally I was grouchy due to my lack of sleep. To try and take my mind off my irritable mood, I went for a horse ride after work for about an hour by myself. Getting away for a while in the wide-open spaces gave me a chance to clear my head. I rode around Mary's Lake and could feel a sense of serenity surrounded by the loveliness of a peaceful lake. In my searching for answers as to what I wanted to do with my life, I was also missing my family and thinking about home. I headed back to the chalet and read letters I'd received from Robbie V. and my cousin Ricky B. before getting ready for Mass. My parents must have sensed my melancholy disposition because they called me after I returned from my ride. Isn't it funny how one day you can feel on top of the world and on the bottom the next? Why was life such a conundrum? I wondered.

Nancy informed me some of the kids wanted to go dancing that evening at The Rock, and they decided they were going to dress like grungy and unkempt hippies. I wondered whose idea that was, but I think I knew. In a better frame of mind, I decided to go along. All I had to wear was my light-colored jeans, but I did have a loose-fitting peasant top that would work and I tied thick yarn around my forehead and long hair. Nancy had some bell-bottom flowered pants that she only wore around her bedroom for leisure, but she wore them with a scarf tied around her short hair. We both had leather sandals that we could dance in.

We headed off to town with everyone who was going to church since we had to go to Mass in our innovative garb. We laughed and giggled on the drive at our crazy costumes while wondering how we were going to keep a straight face. Although we were self-conscious, most probably wouldn't think twice about what we were wearing. By the time we got to the dance place, we were fairly composed. We probably weren't fooling anyone, but we had fun and fit right in with the other non-conformists. By the time the evening ended, I was thinking I rather preferred this type of dress to the Pop art styles and the white go-go boots. Maybe it was time for a change!

Chapter Eight: Monday, July 22

It would be another week of not getting tips as Nancy and I were back to working the pool and terrace area. After work, Randy, the twenty-six-year-old Baptist youth minister, was going to Denver and took Nancy, Dave, Jeanette and me with him to do some shopping. After dinner, while driving back, we got a mini tour of the capital and the biggest city in Colorado just east of the Front Range of the Rockies. Nicknamed the Mile-High City due to the fact the elevation there was exactly one mile, 5280 feet, above sea level. In the 1850s, Denver was named for Kansas Territorial Governor, James W. Denver, by General William Larimer, a Kansas land developer who founded the town. Only one hundred years after the United States declared their independence from Great Britain, Colorado was admitted to the Union in 1876 as the thirty-eighth state.

While driving back to Estes Park, we listened to the car radio news report on the country's first Special Olympics, which had opened over the weekend at Chicago's Soldier Field. More than a thousand athletes with disabilities would compete in two hundred events. I enjoyed sports and grew up joining in childhood activities like running, swimming in the creek, and climbing trees with my brothers on our small rural farm. There wasn't really much for girls in the way of organized sports at my high school other than intermural volley ball, bowling, and basketball. But my good friends, Becky B. and Teresa C., played partners on the girl's tennis team. I was happy to hear about the interest in allowing girls as well as the disabled to participate in more sporting events.

Arriving back at the chalet, there wasn't much time to spare before the weekly religious group discussions started, so I quickly read a thoughtful letter from my friend Ted A. Tonight we talked about the Vietnam War and how it was justified according to Christian ideals. That was a tough question, and there were lots of different opinions about the necessity of self-defense killing and how long the war should go on. We all knew it was because of the war that President Johnson would not be seeking re-election. Someone in the group mentioned Major Colin Powell had returned to Vietnam for a second tour of duty to look into rumors that war crimes might have been committed by US soldiers near the village of My Lai in March. But what choice did they have but to kill or be killed, I assumed. No one knew what to think any more about trying to stop the spread of communism verses saving the lives of our country men. This war had divided the house, and it was barely left standing, separating the hawk and the dove. All I knew was that the reality of war was loss of human life, and I could not celebrate the victory of those casualties no matter what side they were on. I loved my freedom greatly, but we weren't fighting for liberty in our country. Everyone agreed this war was a great human tragedy, and that killing was basically wrong. We just weren't sure what we could do to help except to continue to pray.

Well, that was a downer, I thought, as I walked back to my room. I couldn't help but think about my good friend Suzie G. who was engaged to another friend of mine from high school and he was in Vietnam. I remember when Bill F. first moved to our town from California and how cute everyone thought he was. I talked to my girlfriends about the topics we discussed in the group session and asked them if they knew anyone who was in Vietnam. It seemed they all had known someone who had lost their life or who had life-threatening injuries. The costly sacrifice they were making was so sad, and they were so young to be involved in this conflict was what we reflected on. I said a little prayer for Bill that night for his safety and well-being.

All day Tuesday at work I was still feeling down about the previous night's conversation, so I was glad to see Wednesday roll around for my day off from cleaning. Steve, this tall, handsome blond who worked at the Trail Ridge Store invited me, Nancy, Jan, and Cathy C. from Centralia, Illinois, to go with him to Cheyenne, Wyoming to the rodeo. The Frontier Days had been the largest outdoor rodeo and western celebration in the country since 1897. Most rodeo events are based on the skills required of the cattle rancher. There were cowboys everywhere at this festive rodeo and a train even transported fans up from Denver's Union Station to see the carousing.

Supporters came from all over the land to watch the bull riding, calf roping, bronc bucking, steer wrestling, barrel racing, and other competitive events and exciting trials.

We all purchased a variety of refreshments including hot dogs, fries, corndogs, fried onion rings, and beverages to take to the grandstand and eat while watching the competition. Steve even bought a funnel cake he shared with all us cowgirls. The show was rather exhilarating as I feared for the lives of some of those guys riding on top the wild Brahmas. The summer rains tried to spoil this sporting contest, but with the hot temperatures, it was not a problem for most of us.

Leaving the rodeo after watching the animals slide around in the mud for a while, we went on into town to find an affordable restaurant for dinner. Native Indian dancers were performing in the streets, and we were distracted while watching these talented performers. The dancers, in their typical Indian costumes were celebrating seventy years of participating in Frontier Days. They even had their own Indian Village campground set up in one corner of the park. Although these ethnic peoples of the Great Plains inhabited a vast area of America at one time, the Cheyenne Indians who settled here came over a hundred years ago to government reservations established by the Treaty of Fort Laramie. I particularly enjoyed seeing the small Indian children dressed up in their colorful powwow shirts, dresses, beaded shoes, and headbands. What a treat!

It seemed like we had been eating all day, but here we were eating again before leaving the capital city of Laramie County and making the two-hour drive back up the mountains to Estes Park. I was actually happy to be headed back home to the chalet; it had become my home away from home for the summer. Already I was feeling somewhat melancholy about how I would

miss my chalet family and friends when I had to return to Missouri the first week in September.

***

The late afternoon rains continued to water the grass and keep this dry climate moistened.

Since Nancy and I were working the outside pool and patio rooms, sometimes we had to dodge the deluges or we wouldn't get done with work early. With the clear evening atmosphere, some of us fair-weather maidens and servers headed out with box lunches to have a picnic dinner and enjoy the outdoors. In the conversation, someone mentioned they had heard on the news that the race riots going on in Cleveland this past week had resulted in the death of four blacks and three police officers. This incident set off forty-eight hours of additional violence, looting, arson fires, and beatings. And here we sat in the peacefulness of the mountains and other neighborhoods in our country where as different as night and day. I had no idea all this was going on without television to inform me, and I wasn't sure if I felt ignorant or blessed or both. I did know something needed to change in our culture or there would be more death and loss.

Despite the troubling news, the talent show went on as usual. Some of us regained our energy with the adrenalin rush of stage fright so Steve, Mike, Nancy, and I headed into town to dance at Jax. Most of the bands that played around here were out of Denver or Colorado Springs. But this particular group was from Lincoln, Nebraska called *J. Harrison B & The Bumbles.* Their name didn't quite fit them because they were an eight-piece rhythm and blues ensemble with a great horn section. From time to time, some of the members left the stage and pranced around on the dance floor. We were so glad we had come out to see and hear this entertaining crowd-pleaser.

***

There was never a dull moment around the chalet, and this time it was with some disgruntled employees who wanted more monetary compensation. For the past few weeks, a couple of the waiters had been talking to everyone about going on strike for more pay. We even had a show of hands at dinner one night, but most of us voted against this walkout. I personally hadn't come here to make a big salary or I would have stayed at home and worked a better paying trade.

I had wanted to get away from home for the summer and experience some place more exciting. These disgruntled waiters talked to Mr. 'D' and he set up a meeting with Mr. James, the chalet owner.

Mr. James agreed to some of the changes that they wanted in working conditions, but no raise in wages was approved. Terje, who had instigated this protest, decided to quit. I assumed because he went to Berkeley, he was used to the more radical demonstrations that most of the rest of us were not. He didn't get his way so he left at the same time Mr. James drove away in his Mercedes.

I told some of the other kids about the great band playing at Jax Snax and we all decided to go back on Friday night since Saturday there was a picnic planned for a big group of guests and we had to stay at the lodge to help. For several hours Saturday afternoon, Nancy and I babysat for twenty youngsters under the age of five. Admittedly, I'm not the most patient person and trying to control all those little ones running here and there was exasperating. I got out some games, and Nancy tried to divert them with her usual clowning around, but all I did was watch the clock till I could get away and go do my laundry. Later that evening, it was square dancing in the barn.

The soap opera saga continued with the "strikers" anarchy. My roommate Lynn had been seeing one of the waiters who had sided with Terje, and he decided to quit and go to California with this rebel. Then Lynn packed up her stuff and left with them. Just like that, I was without a roomie. I liked Lynn and wished her the best, but I was worried for her at the same time.

At church that night, we were informed by the priest that Pope Paul the VI reaffirmed the Catholic Church's opposition to artificial contraception. I just hoped he changed his mind by the time I got married. It'd been a long and emotional weekend; I was ready to turn in after Mass.

Chapter Nine: Monday, July 29

I told Nancy about what had happened with Lynn and she immediately asked if she could move in with me. After work, we transferred all of her personal items into my front room area and reshuffled and rearranged and got everything reorganized. Then we went out back to the rubbish dump to find a couple of boards and some bricks to make a bookshelf in our room. It was fun having Nancy as my roomie since she had better decorating ideas for sprucing up the place. We even went to town and bought some candles to set on the shelves and poster pictures to hang on the walls. Everything looked great! I'd miss Lynn, but Nancy and I were better suited together.

Mike, Nancy, and I helped serve food again at the Lazy B Ranch and stayed to watch their western show. There was a guitarist who entertained us by playing and singing his version of the Intruders song, "Cowboy to Girls" and Eddie Cochran's song, "Summertime Blues." He ended his performance by singing the classical song, "They Call the Wind Mariah." What a fitting reminder of where I was at the moment. I never minded volunteering my time when I got to hear live music. We ended the evening by stopping off at Tony's on the way back to play a game of billiards.

I had enjoyed the Lazy B Ranch gig so much, I talked Gina and her boyfriend into going back with me on Tuesday evening. I convinced them we would be mixing work with pleasure, and I promised them they would love the vocalist. Nancy was not feeling well so she didn't go, but Butch had a friend who came along. Everyone was delighted with the Western show and didn't mind slinging hash and beans to the hungry cowpokes. We even had enough time afterward to go to The Rock and listen to the music of the night. This band played "The Tighten

Up" by Archie Bell and The Drells as we danced a few before calling it a night.

***

Just my luck, my day off was rainy and cold out, so I spent most of the day just resting and catching up on my letter writing. Finally, by late afternoon there was a clearing so Kay, Janet, Gina, and I took a chance and went out for a ride, but we got caught in a thunderstorm and had to race the horses back to the stables. Needless to say, we were drenched and got some good teasing.

July washed away as August moved in like a lion along with my mood swings. Nancy and I tallied up our tips for the month

of July and we had made $41.95, almost exactly what we made in June. After dividing up our earnings, we decided to go spend some money. The weather turned nice again, and after work, Nancy and I made the four-mile walk to the store and back and got some much-needed exercise. Nancy talked at length about how it would be fun to work again together the following summer except to get jobs with room and board overseas and travel around Europe. My parents had taken a two-week trip to Europe a few years back, but I always thought going to other countries was something you did in retirement years not during college years. I couldn't imagine how we would pull this off, but Nancy persuaded me that if we returned to school and got part-time jobs for the year, we could earn enough money to pay for the flight over.

Student-exchange programs also arranged jobs with places to live abroad just like here in the States. Well, I was swayed, and now I had something sensational to look forward to next summer.

We were greeted by Janet and Gina in our room with an apple pie they had taken earlier from the kitchen. What a nice afternoon delight as we helped ourselves to dessert before dinner.

Friday night at the movies and *Where Were You When the Lights Went Out* was playing in the lobby. A group of us girls watched this comedy starring Doris Day, one of my most favorite actresses, about the Northeast blackout in New York City that really happened in 1965. Twenty-five million people lost electricity for several hours. I enjoyed any movie with Doris Day, who is so cute, and she had the most dramatic facial expressions in her acting. After the movie, we were invited to a party at Mike and Rick's cabin where some cannabis reefer madness was going on. It was weird for me since I didn't smoke or drink much so I excused myself and left the lunacy.

Back in my room while getting ready for bed, I wondered if I were too narrow-minded or prudish because I didn't enjoy the kind of parties that everyone else seemed to. It was good that I was getting some exposure to how kids my age behaved away from home so I was not entirely unaware of contemporary activities. I knew I would eventually figure out where I fit in and my place in society. Although I hadn't decided on my college major, I was thinking about sociology and psychology so maybe those studies would help with my dilemma. My dad kept pushing me toward the teaching profession, but I was leaning more toward nursing, but not really sure yet.

There had been a big sales convention going on all week at the lodge, and tonight was the culmination of their meeting. Some of us gals were asked to help serve at the Saturday night buffet because there were over three hundred people attending. We had to dress up, and I even put my hair up for a change. This boisterous bunch of salesmen with their wives got fairly loud and unruly.

They were all celebrating the end of the week with several bottles of wine and other cocktails at each table. After we finished serving, I was more than ready to leave just to get away from the noise. Larry D. from Montgomery City, MO was having a get-together in his cabin, and Dave invited me to go. Dave was such a nice guy I felt sure it would be a harmless party. All we did was sit around talking and listening to records so I was actually glad I went.

What a day we had today! Most of the sales people were so hungover they not only did late check-out, some weren't out of their rooms till after 3:00 p.m. with new guests checking in.

What a nightmare it was toward the end of the afternoon. When we finally finished, I headed out to the pool just to sit and unwind. I'd received several letters that I read while relaxing. One was a wedding invitation from Pat N., the president of my Tri Sigma college sorority. Most of the girls I pledged with in this social club were friends I knew in high school. Except for my big-sis in the group, Meri from Kansas City, MO. Meri was cute and smart, only a year older, and she helped me with my studies at the sorority house on campus. We were becoming close friends.

I also received a letter from Mike who let me know he was planning a road trip out to Estes Park with his friends Dave R.

and Frank S. who had the car they would be driving in. The plan was to come the end of August, and they would do some sight-seeing while camping out for a few days, and then I could ride back with them to Springfield. It was hard to believe I would be going home in only a month from now. *I have to make the most of my time left*, I thought, as I continued reading his letter. This was terrific news since I didn't want my parents to have to drive all the way back out to pick me up, and I wasn't sure how I was getting back home.

Mike was the best kind of friend and one of the funniest guys I had ever met. He kept me in stitches all the time with his quick wit and sometimes sick humor. I met him on a blind double date arranged by a couple of my Catholic grade-school friends, Bob and Martha.

Dinner came and went and we were off to Sunday evening Mass. Going out for ice cream after church was becoming a weekly ritual with this crew. I decided to get one of the Nestles' drumstick sugar cones topped with chocolate bits and peanuts, which I seldom indulged in because they were more expensive and probably more in calories. But everyone knows, "N-E-S-T-L-E-S, Nestles make the very best chocolate" so I guess they could get away with charging more. All was well as the week ended on a sweet note as I licked away on my frozen dessert.

Chapter Ten: Monday, August 5

Payday and Nancy and I were back working the first floor. The overload of last week's work caught up with me, and I was dragging my feet today. After cleaning, I went back to my room to finish reading a book, *The Taste of New Wine* by Keith Miller. It was a spiritual book that Randy had loaned me about how developing a closer relationship with God, would help improve more meaningful, personal relationships with family and friends. The author talked at length about accepting yourself and your imperfections and then you could see God more clearly in all that you do. This was something I needed to apply to my life, but I was still confused. This quest for trying to figure out the meaning of life and what I wanted to do with my life was getting more complicated. I had to stop thinking about it or I was going to cry.

I received an affectionate phone call from warm-natured Ronnie, and he told me about the photos he was taking as his new hobby in photography flourished. He liked sports hunting and animals in the wild were his main subjects. I told him he needed to come out to the Rockies for some great scenic prints with all kinds of wildlife for a photo shoot. Then he told me he would rather use me for a photo shoot. I laughed at his remark as we both knew I was too short to be a model.

I loved fashionable clothes, but modeling was one profession I could not pursue. Speaking of wildlife, I had to hurry and get off the phone due to the commotion in the hallway. There was a chipmunk running around with lots of screaming and panic. I helped corral him and get the little critter back outside. As much as I adored them, we did not need one loose in the dorm.

***

Waking up to a warm and sunny day, there was talk around the chalet about camping out. I'd already committed to helping at the Lazy B Ranch, but I wanted to join the group afterward. At the chuck wagon supper, one of the Indians, dressed in full headdress with beads and feathers, gave Nancy and me bracelets he had made in appreciation for our helping out. While driving back to the chalet, we heard news on the car radio that former Vice-President Richard Nixon had won the nomination for president at the Republican National Convention in Miami Beach, Florida.

With almost twice as many campers than the last group that went, Nancy, Dave, Kay, Mike, Berny, Robert, Valerie, Louie L. from Calhan, and Chris P. from Ault, Colorado, and myself headed up the back hills with our sleeping bags in tow. Needless to say, there was lots of talking, laughing, and joking around till the wee hours. We all loved having Dave come along as he would bring his guitar for singing around the campfire. However, the downside of his being there, he snored like a freight train so I hardly slept at all that night. Thank goodness I had the next day off because I went back to sleep in my own comfy bed at 6:00 a.m. and slept till noon. Getting up to more rain outside, I continued to lounge around the rest of the day.

Later that evening, my suite mates and I went to town to see the movie *Rosemary's Baby*.

This psychological horror film starring Mia Farrow would not have been my pick, but the other three wanted to go. So, I sat through this disturbing movie about a pregnant woman who thought an evil cult wanted to take her baby for use in their rituals. I had another night of tossing and turning as I could not stop thinking about this troubling movie about the devil and demons.

The following day continued with recurrent rain, and Nancy and I got caught in a cloudburst while walking back from town after doing weekly laundry. We managed to catch a ride back to the chalet with some guys from the Wind River Ranch who saved our day. We both had to completely redo our hair for the Thursday night talent show. This, by the way, turned out to be a big success as we made $22.00 in tips the next day. With the

extra money, we treated our dorm mates to another show, only this time I picked a pleasant musical comedy, *Thoroughly Modern Millie* starring Julie Andrews and Mary Tyler Moore. The film was set during the roaring twenties and was about a New York City flapper. This movie I enjoyed and it even won seven Academy awards, including best original song. I slept much better!

***

I didn't usually participate at Saturday night square dance, but this particular evening Ron had a friend visiting, who was a soldier stationed at Fort Carson in Colorado Springs. Bob asked me to dance so instead of watching, I tried really hard to follow the calls and show this army officer a good time. We did enjoy the whirling and twirling, and he asked me to go for a bite to eat at the Dinner Bell so we could talk. He let me know he planned to return to Springfield, MO and teach once he got out of the military. But, with the time he had left, he wanted to see more of the park. After work on Sunday, we drove around the area that I had become so familiar with over the past few months. I was his personal tour guide as I told Bob about some of the history and showed him where to see the best views. We even drove up to Bear Lake, which he agreed was one of the most beautiful places he'd seen. As he gazed across the lake at Longs Peak, I let him know I planned to climb that mountain on my next day off. He was returning the following weekend for another visit, and he looked forward to hearing all about my upcoming experience.

Chapter Eleven: Monday, August 12

A Denver High School student council convention checked in over the weekend, and while Nancy and I worked second floor, we noticed a few notes from some of the high school boys.

They invited us to come back to their rooms after we got off work. Well, we got a good chuckle from their requests, and Nancy replied to one of the notes that our coming back would require a bigger tip than they could afford. Besides, we already had plans to serve at the Lazy B Ranch after work. Randy, Doug, and George W. from Princeton, Kentucky joined Nancy and me for what seemed like a second job for us. We did have fun and usually went home with a gift. This time we were given a dozen leftover, homemade buttermilk biscuits that we shared with everyone.

Tuesday at work some of the high school boys in one of the rooms asked for some extra soap. My scheming-minded, cleaning partner proceeded to place the mini-sized bars of soap not only in the bathroom but everywhere. Nancy would do things that I would be worried about getting in trouble over, but she found it to be hilarious. She placed soap on the beds, under the pillows, in their coat pockets, and behind the curtains. Speaking of partners, I shared a letter with Nancy that I had received from Lynn, letting me know they had made it to California and all was well.

After dinner, I stayed in for the evening because as long as it didn't pour down rain the next day, I would be climbing Longs Peak, the highest of the park's 113 named mountains, with Pam, Sue, Berny, David, Terry G. from Boulder, CO, and his girlfriend Patsy. All of my unquestioning roommates gave me lots of encouragement and reassurance since none of us had any idea what I was getting myself into. I did know that the sixteen-mile, round-trip undertaking could take twelve hours of endurance. I was acclimated to the elevation in Estes Park, but we would be gaining about five thousand more feet. Nancy, Gina, Janet, and I played cards on my bed in our room till I told them I needed to get some shut eye for my big day ahead. They wished me good luck.

***

I was up at 4:30 a.m. and met everyone in the lobby at five as we drove to the base of where we started our climb at about nine thousand feet. Even though technical equipment was not needed for this late summer climb over the North Face Cable route, we did register at the entrance of the trailhead. The first recorded climb was made in 1868. Early mornings were cool, and I was glad to have my heavy coat, but after a while, I got warm and had to take it off. Terry carried our food and supplies in his backpack. Most of the way I enjoyed the walk as we made the ascension through the established traversing trails until we reached the boulder fields. Tall, self-assured Terry cautioned us, since he had climbed this peak before, that this section would be a challenge.

We literally had to climb over this huge rock slide in a massive field of giant boulders. I tried to jump from one rock to another but fell and hit my shinbone so hard I swear I heard it crack. My leg swelled and turned black and blue, but despite the pain, I was still able to walk. As I limped along, all I could think about was getting to the top. I was determined, now that we had made it thus far. It was eight miles up, and we still had probably another mile to go on this rigorous part.

At the end of the boulder field came another test of my fortitude. Although Terry had briefed us about what this climb required in the way of strength and endurance, I had never undertaken such a strenuous task. It was a good thing I was raised as somewhat of a "tomboy" and in fairly good physical condition. We reached the cable climb, which went straight up the side of a solid rock formation. *You have got to be kidding,*

I thought, as I looked up at what I would have to do next. The heavy-duty steel rope tow was already secured in the rocks, and it was our mission to hold on to the cable and pull ourselves up while finding a crevice in the rocks for foot holds. Terry went first to demonstrate how it was done, followed by Berny and Dave. Then we girls climbed, and I was the last to make it to the top. What a relief once we all made it up. It was definitely cold at the highest elevation, and I was certainly glad to have my coat on at the peak point. Then Pam initiated some individual and group photo takes on top of the summit.

The air was dangerously thin at over fourteen thousand feet, and I wasn't sure if my headache was from lack of oxygen or nourishment. It was close to noon and weather clouds were not looking good, but we made time for a quick lunch break before heading back down the other side of the peak.

Just as we started the descent, it commenced to snow. It wasn't long before the heavy white stuff was coming down so hard I could barely see a few feet in front of me. We were way above the tundra with no ground underfoot but steep rock cliffs that were getting slick fast from the ice.

I slipped at one point and started to fall, and if Berny, my confident savior, had not grabbed my arm, it could have been disastrous. Red-headed Terry warned us that people had died climbing this mountain. I was beginning to wonder why I had come as the strong winds began blowing so hard I could barely move from the cold in this blizzard. Injured, scared, and afraid I would fall again, I just sat down and slid on the slippery, flat solid rocks until I regained enough confidence to walk again.

Finally, we made it to the tree line and there was soil to walk on and small bushes and trees to grab hold of. Then the snow turned to rain, and now I was freezing from the moisture and no hat on my head. The cloth-knit gloves I had brought in the pocket of my coat were wet and soggy and not much use. I was too cold to talk but not too cold to pray as we kept moving down the hillside.

It was hard to stay on course so what should have been an eight-mile hike turned to ten miles.

The rain persisted most of the way back, and by the time we reached the bottom at 4:30 p.m. in the afternoon, we were all soaking wet and pretty miserable. On the drive back to the chalet, I kept wondering about my sanity and that of everyone else who had attempted this climb to the top of the world.

Since John Wesley Powell completed the trek one hundred years earlier, men and women have continued to be foolish about climbing these difficult and sometimes treacherous mountains.

Though exhausted physically, mentally, and emotionally, the mountain forever bears my name.

Back at the lodge, all I wanted to do was take a long hot bath to get my body temperature and composure back to normal. I couldn't even talk about my big adventure because my lips wouldn't move. At dinner, I was able to discuss the day's event and share my thoughts and feelings about the climb. David M. from Paonia, Colorado asked me if I would do it again, knowing what I would have to go through, and I replied without any hesitation, "Probably not!"

My whole body ached the next morning, even my bottom side as I rolled on to the floor out of bed. Making beds helped work out the kinks, and by late afternoon, I was feeling my usual self again and even went horseback riding with some of the girls. August 15 was a holy day of obligation for the Catholics, the feast of the Assumption of Mary, so several of us headed to Mass after dinner.

As we commemorated the end of Mary's earthly life before going up to heaven, I was happy to still be on Earth and thanked God for sparing my life after yesterday's frightening ordeal.

Later in the evening, as my roommates and I played Category Challenge, we could hear some hubbub going on in the hallway so we paused our game. This time it was a bird that had flown through a window, and the lark was dodging in and out of rooms as we hurriedly opened all the windows in hopes he would find a way out. After all the racket and interruption, we returned to the board game after our feathered friend exited out an opening. I was never too crazy about board games, and I decided it was probably due to my impatience of waiting for my turn to play.

Ron's friend, Bob, returned to Estes Park for the weekend as promised so I accompanied him again as he explored the area. Saturday afternoon, we drove to Grand Lake, stopping on the way at Trail Ridge store to eat dinner. While walking around the lake, we ran into a sorority sister of mine, Cheryl C. and her boyfriend Jim R. from Springfield. *What a small world after all*, I thought, but then again, this was a popular destination for the whole world. As the long day turned into night, we drove back to the chalet and square-danced with the others in the lobby.

Sunday afternoon, Bob and I took a picnic lunch and walked up a small mountain trail so we could sit and take in the views. Before the hike, we drove into town to pick up my pictures so

I could show him what I went through as I told him all about the Longs Peak escapade. I laughed about what we had done as I revisited my almost tragic incident. After eating, I took Bob with me to the Lazy B Ranch, and we watched the show and ate together after I helped serve the dinners.

When we returned to the chalet, I think Bob sensed I had no desire for a physical relationship with anyone at the time. Getting through college and figuring out a career were my main focus. I cherished male friendships as I thanked him and wished him the best before saying goodbye.

Chapter Twelve: Monday, August 19

We had come full circle as Nancy and I were back working north wing where we began the first of the summer. It was getting close to contract completions for many of the employees who had to return to their respective colleges. Nancy would be leaving at the end of the week, and I was already feeling gloomy. Nancy's parents were here for the week to vacation, and they would head home with Nancy on Sunday. In fact, after work Nancy's parents took us into town to buy a cake for Mike's going-away party and some goodies for George as he was leaving soon. We also let them buy a bottle of Scotch for Berny's birthday coming up. The party was bittersweet!

A band called Eric and the Norsemen from Lawrence, Kansas were staying at the chalet for the week. I met founding member and guitarist Mike 'Rolph' Willman and lead singer Roger Johnson, while cleaning their room. They quizzed me about what there was to do around the chalet, and I told them about Bear Lake and Trail Ridge Road and invited them to ride horses with me after work. To my surprise, several more members of the band, organist Mitch Bible, drummer Jim Kocher, and bass players Frank Berrier and Forest 'Tree' Cloud, came with Mike and Roger to the stables to ride or just to watch. I quickly got the impression these guys, who started playing together at college a few years back, were best of friends as they teased and laughed at one another. The ride was too funny with these inexperienced cowboy musicians.

Roger asked me to go out dancing later, but I had already promised my time to the Lazy B Ranch so he went with me to see the Western show, and then we joined the other band members at The Rock for some late-night rock-n-roll. Roger told me their band also played the latest hits with a few original songs thrown into the mix. I was thinking to myself that I would love to hear them play, and then he told me they were on stage at Grand Lake Lodge for one of their last concerts Thursday night if I wanted to come up and listen. That sounded like a great idea to me!

Several of us gals were up early for a road trip to Denver. Nancy, Pam, Cathy, Mike, and I piled into Valerie's car and headed first to the airport to drop off Mike, who was flying back to Oklahoma on Frontier Airlines. As we all hugged and waved farewell to our good-natured Mike, I felt this overwhelming sense of sadness. I suppose I had never known such happiness, freedom, and pure joy of living while working and playing with all these kids that I would probably never see again. I could feel tears forming up in my eyes.

We drove away from Stapleton International Airport and on to a brand-new shopping mall called Cinderella City in the suburb of Englewood. I had never seen such a fine-looking center that donned an exquisite fountain as you entered to go to the four different sections. One of the two basement corridors simulated a New York City street complete with outdoor facades and streetlamps. Eating dinner here was like being out for a "night on the town." I didn't buy much, but I certainly did enjoy walking around window gawking.

As we left the largest covered shopping mall west of the Mississippi, we drove on to the heart of Denver's history where the legendary Larimer Square was located. Here there was a collection of restaurants, night spots, galleries, and shops in a mid-Victorian setting. Supposedly this was where Denver founder General Larimer built his cabin at Fifteenth and Larimer in 1858. It had only been a few years ago that a group of Denver people started this project of preserving some of the original sites built in the 1860s by adding gaslights, courtyards, and the gayety of Denver's heyday.

Also, it was a place where the hippies hung out, so we got an eye full while watching the hippy girls in their see-through blouses and the long-haired guys dawning the peace sign to bystanders.

The jam-packed day of amusement came to an end as we headed back to Estes Park with a drive through Boulder so Pam and Cathy could see this university that had been around since the founding of the state of Colorado. As we listened to music on the car radio, the news reported that the Soviet Union had invaded Czechoslovakia, halting Prague's campaign and the protestors against communism. Over 130 civilians were killed and 500 others injured. It was a good thing we got occasional updates on the car radio or I would have had no idea what was going on in the rest of the world. For most of us, working at the chalet these past three months had been like living in a treasure chest box full of daily excitement. But the reality of our heaven on earth would soon be coming to an end as I was reminded by the despairing broadcast.

***

Riding up to Grand Lake Lodge in a caravan with Eric and the Norsemen, I eagerly waited for evening when I got to see these band members in concert. They could not have been a nicer bunch of guys! Even Al "Stamper" Lewis, the road manager, treated me like I was a celebrity.

Feeling rather special, I got to hang around this semi-famous band and follow them for a day as a groupie. After we all ate dinner, the party started while we watched what turned out to be "The Wildest Show in the Midwest." They were named this by fans in Kansas, and it was really true. Roger never stopped moving, as he sang, shouted, danced, jumped, and played his guitar and horns while performing. He was a natural showman as the rest of the band worked hard to complement his efforts. They were extremely talented, and I loved spending the day with them.

However, I decided traveling with a band was not what I ever wanted to do again. By the time the party ended and they had packed up their instruments and equipment, it was three in the morning before we headed back over the pass only to be slowed down by a summer snowstorm. We got back at 5:00

a.m., allowing me maybe an hour of sleep before I had to be up for work, as the band members slept on. They had to leave mid-day so I would miss seeing them off. At least I didn't have to exert myself much at work. Quiet Louie, the house boy, left for home so Mrs. Mosley had Nancy and me drive the old pick-up truck, transporting dirty linens to the laundry facilities.

Friday night and I was laying low. After dinner, I talked to all my buddies as they began cleaning out their dressers and packing up some of their stuff to head home on Sunday. I was so tired I could barely keep my eyes open, but it was hard to sleep with all the banging around of suitcases and boxes they had to fill. We would all go home with much more than we came with.

Nancy and I split the $51.20 in tips we had made so far this month and then I tried going to sleep.

***

On this last day of cleaning for my three roomies, after work we exchanged gifts with each other. Nancy gave me a stunning turquoise-colored candle to go with my new jewelry. More hugs and tears resulted as we expressed our gratefulness for the opportunity to get to know one another during this magical summer of fun and friendship. It made me think of the ending to the movie *The Wizard of Oz* as Dorothy said goodbye to her three new friends, but she liked one more than the others and Nancy was that person for me. My only comfort was, if all went well, I would see Nancy again the following summer. We headed off to a dinner party at the buffet for Mrs. Mosley and Mrs. Maps. The maids presented them both with bouquets of yellow roses.

My three suite mates left early Sunday morning, leaving me alone for the next two weeks or so I thought. I didn't even have a record player anymore to spin my easy listening tunes on. Jeannette and I were paired up together so I got to know her a little better. She was actually the youngest girl working there, a recent high school graduate. One of ten kids from a large Catholic family, the whole household resided in Estes Park for the summer. They had also lived in Paris a few years because of her dad's occupation, and she could speak fluent French. I told her about the plan that Nancy came up with to try and get jobs and work overseas if possible.

The dorm room was much quieter now but much easier to clean with half the junk gone that was all over the floors, walls, and exposed closet space. As I looked at my scarcely clad figure in the full-length mirror on the back of the door, I made up my mind to shed the six or eight pounds I had gained on my summer vacation before going back to Missouri. It would be easier not to eat so much without the other girls around. The room had been decluttered, and I needed to do the same to my physique. I wrote a few letters before heading off to Mass with only half of the group that usually went. There was a leather-goods store close to the church, and I picked up a carved wrist band for myself and some watch bands for my brothers as last-minute gifts.

Chapter Thirteen: Monday, August 26

Back working the pool area, Sharon would be my partner. Since I was one of the few girls who could drive a standard car with a clutch, I continued to drive the four-on-the-floor truck delivering the dirty laundry. My older brother Chuck had a VW Bug (Volkswagen) and he had taught me how to drive the stick shift. We ran into Nila and Liz V. from Dilworth, MN who told me they were moving into Janet and Gina's vacant room. They lived in the floor above us and Mrs. Mosley wanted everyone to move to the lower floor so she could clean the upper dorms.

After work, with the help of Karen and Edgen G. from Mogadore, Ohio, I acquired a couple of new occupants. Lois would be moving into Nancy's side of the apartment soon. While visiting with everyone in my room, I was interrupted by a phone call from Mike, who was checking about last-minute trip plans and confirming my departure day. Although my contract date didn't end till September 7, Mike wanted to head back on the third if I could get away early.

The conversations were different now with my three new suit mates. I didn't know them as well, but they were fun to hang out with. We all made a trip into town after work to buy last-minute gifts to take home. I was quickly depleting the money I had tried to save for next summer.

On the way back to the chalet, we heard The Beatles newest record release "Hey Jude," which was a really, really long, seven-minute song. But I liked most anything they sang!

The movie *Second Time Around*, a Western comedy starring Debbie Reynolds was showing in the lobby, which we went down to watch. Debbie, another one of my favorite actresses, played a widow who moved her family from New York to the Arizona Territory in 1911. When I was a little girl, I had wanted to grow up and be just like Debbie Reynolds. I even made a scrapbook of her with pictures I cut out of my aunt's movie magazines I was so obsessed by her charm and talent.

Checking with Mr. Davidson about leaving a few days early, he changed my separation date. On my day off, there was no one available to spend time with me on a beautiful sunny day. Only a few days earlier, the temperature had been freezing out, and today it was back up in the eighties.

Due to the mostly rainy summer, I decided to work on my faded tan, but the pool was so crowded I devised another plan for sunning. Climbing out the window in our dorm room, I went out on the flat part of the roof to lie in the sun. I almost got away with it, but Mrs. Mosley saw me up there and waved me to get down. She was not very happy with my unconventional sun bathing.

I opted instead to write a long letter to my childhood friend from Muskogee and tell Melody all about my incredible summer in Colorado and what I hoped to do with my summer in '69.

Later on, we gals went into town to see yet another movie, *For Love of Ivy*, starring Sidney Poitier and Abbey Lincoln. This romantic comedy about a black domestic maid was a show we could all relate to as she wanted to leave her cleaning job and go to secretarial school to improve her situation. None of us gals watching the show wanted to be career "Merry Maids," and most of us would soon be returning to school to improve our current lot in life.

***

The week was quickly passing by, and once again Jeannette and I went into town with her brother to spend more money. I wanted to buy a pair of lederhosen. Living in this alpine region made me think of the Swiss Alps, which I hoped to see by this time next year, and I just had to have those green leather shorts. On the way back to the chalet, listening to the car radio, we heard that police and National Guardsmen went on a rampage, breaking up antiwar demonstrators at the Democratic National

Convention in Chicago. Even in our own country there was violence in the streets. Vice-President Hubert Humphrey had won
the Democratic nomination for president.

Back at the chalet, I was still getting letters from home,
and I even received an unexpected note from Roger Johnson
who let me know "There's no place like home" as he and all
the band members had made it back safely to Kansas. They
stopped in Abilene to play their last gig before the band split
up. He apologized for getting me home so late the night after
the Grand Lake concert. I was just glad we had made it home
with the top of Trail Ridge Road turning so cold and treacherous. They had no idea that the pass had been closed that
morning due to all the accumulated snow, and we were driving
through that mess.

Regrettably, the remaining working maids decided not to perform in the talent show since so many of our group were absent.
Many of the waiters had gone too, but the few left dressed up
for the amateur night in their hilarious hats, scarfs, vests, and
sunglasses and sang The Byrd's song "I'll Feel a Whole Lot Better." I sat and watched the show with everyone else and laughed
at all those guys I called friends who had been strangers not so
long ago. I almost cried as I listened to Pat N. from Bloomington,
IL. sing "The Impossible Dream." Maybe this was because living out here had been like a dream and I was about to wake-up.
Nevertheless, in these past few months I'd learned that nothing is
impossible, proving it to myself by climbing Long's Peak. After
the show, Randy, Dave, Robert, Berny, Kay, Mary C. from Glen-
view, IL., and I went dancing at The Rock one last time.

The lingering days were slowing down, but a full house was
expected Labor Day weekend.

I got off early on another cloudy day so I packed all the
things in my room that I was taking back to Missouri except
my clothes. My Chanel No. Five perfume was missing, which
annoyed me, but I could hardly accuse someone in my room
of taking my cologne. With no plans for the evening, Jeannette
and I went to see another movie. *Far from the Madding Crowd*
was a British epic drama set in nineteenth-century rural England

82

starring Julie Christie. The Victorian era film was about an independently minded woman who inherits her uncle's farm as class distinctions and social codes still surrounded the characters. It was an interesting show!

On this last day of the month, I started off cleaning my rooms by walking in on a man in his underwear. I was so embarrassed and could do nothing but apologize, but I had knocked before I opened the door. This seemed to set my mood for the rest of the day as I just wanted to forget about what had happened. After dinner, Cherry B. from Denver invited all the gals left in the dorm to a going-away party upstairs in an empty storage area that could house a large group of invitees. She had snacks and one of the older guys bought some hard liquor for her. I decided I wanted to know what it was like to get drunk and feel this "buzz" that everyone talked about. I commenced to drink vodka and orange juice so rapidly that I got totally smashed very quickly.

The next thing I remembered was waking up in my bed sick as a dog. I had no idea how I had gotten there, and I could not recollect anything about the party. I do recall spending a good deal of time looking at the toilet bowl while sitting on the bathroom floor. I tried going to work, but after a few hours, I had to excuse myself and go back to bed. I was so dizzy I even thought maybe I had a touch of the flu. The one thing I did learn from this abuse of alcohol was I would never do it again. There was nothing fun about it because I couldn't remember anything that happened.

By late afternoon, I started feeling normal again and welcomed my friends Mike, David, and Frank, who arrived from Missouri around five o'clock. The chalet was crowded with people for the annual Labor Day picnic so we drove into town in Frank's green Firebird and had dinner before going to Sunday evening Mass. Back at the chalet, the guys set up a campsite for sleeping and I stayed out with them by the campfire to visit and catch up on what was happening in Springfield.

***

My last day to work was appropriately named Labor Day. Few folks were checking out due to the holiday so it was not crazy busy like most Mondays. When I picked up my last pay-check, I began my goodbyes to management and staff members who were hanging around the lobby. I thanked everyone for the best summer of my life and told them that the excitement of work-ing here had ruined me because it would be hard to return to my ordinary life back in Missouri. The mountains, the scenery, the experiences, and even all the rain would bring me back someday.

Mike, David, Frank, and I drove to Trail Ridge Store so they could see some of the sites and appreciate a little more why I loved working in the Rocky Mountains. Returning to the chalet, we loaded my things in the trunk of Frank's car and were barely able to fit it all in. Then we went to Tony's for pizza and in to

Estes Park for ice cream as we walked along the meandering creek that flows behind the shops. The last dancing I did in Estes Park was with my Missouri guys.

We had a long, ten-hour drive back to Springfield. Piling into the car early Tuesday morning, I waved to the chalet as we drove away for the last time from the amazing neighborhood that I had worked and played in during my extraordinary summer in '68. Priceless!

***

To quote William Shakespeare, "Parting is such sweet sorrow," and it was for me as I returned to resume life again with my family and friends back home. Growing up in the sixties and all that it entailed, whether living in a big city, Vietnam, or wide-open places connected us all together.

Maybe it had something to do with the clothes, the music, the general feeling at the time that we youth of the Kennedy Generation were chosen by destiny. We had the world by the tail, and we were going to make a difference in the future of our country. All these things were rolled up into one big, colorful ball, and even with all the good, bad, and ugly that may have occurred during that summer, these were the ingredients that made up the camaraderie and youthful elation of a time, no matter where it was spent, as we all lived our lives through a summer that changed the world.

Epilogue

On returning to college in the fall of 1968, I soon discovered my attitude about living at home was worse than before. I managed to get a part-time evening job so I could afford to move into my sorority house for the semester. I lived with five roommates, and by the next semester, four of us had moved into an apartment close to campus where we continued to share expenses. The war in Vietnam raged on and we got word that our friend Bill Fishback was killed on September 9.

With the money I made at work, I even went back out to Winter Park, Colorado over semester break with a bus load of students on a ski trip. For the first few days, I was awkward and hated this winter sport, but by day three, I was beginning to get the feel of shifting my weight on the downhill turns and decided I might like this thrilling winter sport after all.

I also managed to save enough money for the trip to Europe the following summer, but Nancy backed out last minute. She and Stan had decided to get married, and unfortunately, I lost touch with them. My good friends Meri and Melody stepped up to accompany me on my adventure. It was similar to my delightful summer in Estes Park, only Europe turned into dozens more delights with a diverse variety of scenery, tastes, smells, and sights. And now fifty years have passed in a blink!

However, I remember my summer at the Estes Park Chalet as being unforgettable. Maybe it was because of living away from home and doing so much in such a short amount of time. I shared first time experiences like hitch-hiking, mountain climbing, getting drunk, and I survived it to do it all over again. It's hard to place a value on what I learned, but I do recall going home more confident and knowledgeable. Everyone has a story to tell about life's lessons and how it affects who they eventually become. I've been blessed with many such stories!

Ten years after the summer of 1968, there was a devastating fire in the kitchen at the Estes Park Chalet, and most of the south wing of the lodge was destroyed. For many years, it was abandoned and passed through several ownerships until 1999 when it was extensively renovated and renamed Mary's Lake Lodge. For several years, the lodge struggled to make a comeback, but in recent years, it has been fully restored to its original mountain destination.

After college and marriage, I continued traveling to Colorado and took my three young children, Tara, Natalie, and Ryan, on ski vacations over the Christmas holidays. I wanted to introduce them to the Rockies that I still get excited about every time I see the mountains. In fact, two of my adult children settled there after finishing school. Then after my divorce in 1997, I grabbed the opportunity to move to Vail Valley Colorado and lived there for seven fabulous years. In the summer of 2003, I visited the former Estes Park Chalet for the first time in thirty-five years.

This time I celebrated my birthday as a paying guest. As I entered the restored but familiar lobby with a good friend, nostalgic memories resurfaced of a former time gone by. Much of the lodge had been remodeled and updated, but much was left the same. I even walked up to where the girl's dormitory was and those rooms had been modified and refurbished for renting to visitors.

I left Colorado in 2004 after realizing that some of that blissful "Rocky Mountain high" was actually referring to the skyrocketing cost of living in a prosperous resort town. Like many of the baby-boom generation, I got to experience a new kind of high that was like no other, my first perfect grandchild came into my life. God was always with me through all my ups and downs.

I would be remiss not to mention that even with the highs and lows of everyday life, I always found hope in every situation, despite those times in life when my happy persona retreated back into its shell. My life has not always been easy, but it has been good. I've been lucky to have a good family, good health, and good friends that no amount of money could ever buy.

The only possible advice I have to offer to anyone out there reading this book: don't be afraid to let a little sunshine into your life from time to time. It helps you see more clearly!

About the Author

Marianne Davidson was born in Tulsa, Oklahoma in 1949. Early in life, her oldest brother nicknamed her Deedee, which she has used all her life. Growing up in Springfield, MO, Dee graduated from Glendale High School in 1967 (when she shortened her name to Dee). She earned degrees in sociology in 1971 and secondary guidance and counseling in 1979 at SMS, Southwest Missouri State University. Working in sales and the medical field for over twenty-five years, she is now the retired mother of three adult children and five charming grandchildren.

Spirited and energetic, Dee has accomplished everything she ever made up her mind to do from skydiving to scuba diving and everything in between. An avid runner for twenty years, she ran a marathon at the age of forty-eight. She's spent many years living in and visiting the lovely mountain states of Colorado and Washington, and she took advantage of all the sports opportunities those areas had to offer from skiing, biking, hiking, and climbing. Traveling overseas numerous times, she published a book about her first trip abroad, *A Summer in '69* when she and two girlfriends hitchhiked their way through more than a dozen European countries.

Dee currently lives in Springfield with her husband, Dr. John D. Hume. She keeps busy with several genealogical societies and volunteers at her Catholic Church community as well as at the History Museum on the Square. Her travels today consist mostly of visiting family in Denver and Seattle as well as senior bus trips. She especially enjoys summer boating with family and friends at her cabin on beautiful Table Rock Lake in Branson, Missouri.

Review Requested:
If you loved this book, would you please provide a review at Amazon.com?

CPSIA information can be obtained
at www.ICGtesting.com
Printed in the USA
FSHW02n2345280918
52400FS